# EASY ENTERTAINING

## successful party food and drinks

Edited by Jackie Cunningham-Craig

Distributed by Roydon Publishing Company Limitec
81 Goswell Road
London EC1V 7ER

Published by Marshall Cavendish Books Limited
58 Old Compton Street
London W1V 5PA



Printed and bound by L.E.G.O., Vicenza, Italy

ISBN 0 946674 85X

# CONTENTS

# SPIRITS AND COCKTAILS

There are a great many spirits in the world. But what we now normally call spirits embrace the five in widespread everyday use – whisky, gin, vodka, rum and brandy. And for present purposes, we are applying the word 'cocktail' to some mixed drinks – long and short – associated with these principal spirits. They're well worth the time if you have flourish and panache. Just flick through the pages and start making them today.

## Spirits

Spirits are produced by distillation: from a mildly alcoholic liquor, the alcohol is collected and concentrated. Alcohol vaporizes at 78.3°C [172.4°F] and water at 100°C [212°F]. Theoretically you have only to bring the original brew to 78.3°C [172.4°F] to separate the alcohol from the water. Basic distillation can take place in the traditional pot-still, or in a more complicated patent-still, where distillation can happen continuously.

## Cocktails

When cocktails are not made in the glass from which they will be drunk, most cocktails can be, and many should be, mixed: drinks containing heavy cordials

improve by being shaken in a cocktail shaker (though it's not essential). Use ice generously in all cases, except where stated. In the following recipes, numbers refer to quantities of a measure, or fractions of it: a measure is a standard 25 ml/1 fl oz jigger.

# WHISKY AND WHISKEY

### Whisky, Scotch

This is the world's most prestigious and internationally-enjoyed spirit. The art of distilling came to Scotland with Christian monks from Ireland at an early date. Whisky was known to the Scottish Royal Court in Edinburgh in 1500. It had a turbulent social history. It was a cottage industry: most crofters were distillers. Efforts to control and tax production, especially in the Highlands, were notably unsuccessful till the 1820s. Scotch whisky was little appreciated in England, except in the extreme north, until the introduction in the 1860s of blended whisky, combining the robustness of malt whisky with the blandness of grain whisky. Rather less than a century ago, pioneer Scottish blenders started onslaughts on the English – and later the world – market which proved immensely successful. Malt whisky is made by allowing barley briefly to sprout, the water used being of prime importance. The malted barley is dried by peat fires: this is vital. It is then coarsely ground. Hot water is added and from this mash a sweetish liquid (wort) is drawn.

Yeast is added to the wort, which ferments, and this becomes the alcoholic wash (about 10% alcohol). The wash goes into a pot-still. The resultant spirit (low wines) is transferred into another and similar still, which produces malt whisky. It is matured in oak casks for a legal minimum of three years, but normally considerably longer.

Grain whisky is produced by the patent-still process and is rarely matured beyond the legal minimum. It is used for marrying with malt whisky to produce the many brands of blended scotch whisky which represent about 95% of all Scotch whisky sold. Scotch whisky averages about 50% of malt and grain.

The number of individual malts in a good blend can be as many as sixty: in the case of lesser brands it may only be a fraction of good malt to give character and a very high percentage of grain.

### Whiskey, Irish

This has greatly lost popularity although it's enjoying a mild resurgence of interest through Irish coffee. Whiskey was, in legend at least, distilled in Ireland 1,000 years ago. In Eire distilling is concentrated in the hands of an amalgamation of the three main distilleries. In Ulster there is only one distillery, the famous Bushmills. The mash for Irish whiskey is barley (usually only half of it is malted), wheat, rye and – peculiar to Ireland – oats. Pot-stills are used, and three separate distillations. Irish whiskey is distinctively more pungent than blended Scotch. It has by law to be matured for seven years.

### Whisky, American

The law specifies 30 type of American whisky, but only one name is protected by Act of Congress – bourbon. This is the type mostly known overseas.

Bourbon is made from a mash containing not less than 51% corn (maize). (Rye whisky has a mash of a minimum of 51% rye). American whisky must be distilled at comparatively low strength and matured in new casks, which means that bourbon is rather highly flavoured. After much agitation, a major US whisky company gained federal approval to distil an American 'light' whisky at a higher strength and to mature in previously used casks.

### Whisky, Canadian

This is the fourth important regional whisk(e)y. Canadian whisky is made from a mash mostly of corn, with rye, wheat and some malted barley. Patent- rather than pot-still distillation is the rule, and the whisky tends to be light in flavour; perhaps the best description of it is that it is half way between Scotch and the better American rye whiskies. It is widely distributed in Britain and even more so in the USA.

## Whisky cocktails

### Atholl Brose

1½ Scotch;
1 each pure cream and clear honey. Mix in warm glass. Allow to cool. *Or* omit cream and top with hot milk.

### Blood and Sand

½ each Scotch, cherry brandy, fresh orange juice, sweet vermouth. Shake. Strain into adequate glass.

### Bobby Burns

1½ Scotch; ¾ sweet vermouth; a teaspoon of Benedictine. Stir. Strain into cocktail glass. Squeeze lemon rind over.

### Rob Roy

½ each Scotch and sweet vermouth. Shake.

### Whisky Mac

Equal proportions Scotch and ginger wine. No ice.

### Toddy

Teaspoon sugar in warm glass, dissolved with little boiling water; 2 Scotch. Stir, top with boiling water and add more Scotch to taste.

### Rusty Nail

Half-and-half Scotch and Drambuie, 'on the rocks' with twist of lemon.

### Manhatten

1 bourbon; ½ each dry and sweet vermouth; dash angostura bitters. Stir. Strain into cocktail glass. Add cocktail cherry.

### Old Fashioned

In a small tumbler, a teaspoon of sugar; 3 dashes angostura; 3 ice cubes; 2 bourbon (or Canadian).

### Serpent's Tooth

1 Irish 2 sweet vermouth; 1 lemon juice; ½ kümmel, dash angostura. Stir. Strain.

# GIN

For practical purposes this means the London dry gin type, made all over the world, but generally conceded to be at its finest when the production of a handful of London-based firms of some antiquity; the oldest dates from 1740. Dry gin evolved from unsweetened gin, brought in about 100 years ago in contrast to sugary cordial 'Hollands' or 'Old Tom'. Gins vary greatly in taste – and often in quality.

There are many practical short cuts to making gin. At its best it will be based on a pure neutral spirit. This spirit will be rectified (re-distilled) which further purifies it and this may be why that connoisseur of good living, the late André Simon, classified gin as 'the purest of all spirits'. This rectified spirit is flavoured by various methods with salubrious juniper. This is essential to all true gin; the name is a corruption of the old Dutch genever (geneva) – juniper. Oil of juniper has long been valued medically. Another ingredient is coriander, and there are further botanical ingredients in use; their numbers and proportions form the closely guarded formulae of the distillers.

Gin is now in universal use, but only comparatively lately has it become respectable for a drink for women as well as men. In its earlier history gin was associated with working-class drunkeness and, especially in London, was imbibed in vast quantities – often illicitly distilled. Perhaps the coming of the Cocktail Age (a spin-off from Prohibition in the USA) did as much as anything to make gin fashionable as opposed to popular.

The other main gin, once much drunk in England, is Dutch (geneva) gin. This is much more pungent than London dry gin and is for drinking chilled and straight.

Plymouth gin, a famous proprietary brand from the city, has a particular association with Pink Gin (gin with a touch of angostura).

## Gin-based cocktails

Most of the 'classic' cocktails that have stood the test of time were based on dry gin.

### Dry Martini
2 gin; ¼ dry vermouth (or less in modern use). Stir. Strain. Squeeze lemon rind over, not immersing. Olive optional.

### Clover Club
1 gin; ½ grenadine syrup; juice ½ lemon; white of 1 egg. Shake briskly. Strain.

### Gibson
As Dry Martini but with a cocktail onion instead of an olive.

### Gimlet
Half-and-half gin and lime juice cordial. Stirred, shaken, 'on the rocks' with or without a splash of soda.

### Gin Fizz
1 gin; juice ½ lemon; ½ tablespoon powdered sugar. Shake. Strain. Add soda.

### Gin Rickey
2 gin 'on the rocks'; ½ teaspoon grenadine; juice ½ lemon which is then crushed into drink. (Rickeys may be made with other spirits).

### Gin Sling
Juice 1 lemon; heaped teaspoon sugar; 2 gin; dash angostura; 'on the rocks' with a little water.

### Horse's Neck
Hang spiral of lemon peel in tall glass; 2 gin (or other spirit); top with dry ginger ale.

### Silver Streak
1 gin on the rocks; ½ each lemon juice and kümmel.

### Collins
As Gin Sling, but soda instead of water.

### White Lady
½ gin; ¼ each lemon juice and cointreau; teaspoon egg white (optional). Shake. Strain.

### Trinity
1 each gin, sweet vermouth, dry vermouth. Mix. Strain.

*Horse's Neck* · *Blood and Sand* · *Bullshot* · *Dry Martini* · *Champagne Cockta[il]*

# VODKA

This can mean two things. There are Russian or Polish vodkas, of various types but usually delicately flavoured. These are best drunk very cold and neat as an accompaniment to tasty tidbits.

But for most people, vodka means the Anglo-American spirit that is as lacking in taste as it is possible for a spirit to be.

The term Anglo-American is used advisedly: the modern vogue for vodka drinking started in the USA and can actually be pin-pointed to the Cock 'n Bull Tavern, Los Angeles, where was invented the 'Moscow Mule' (vodka, iced ginger beer and lime or lemon juice). The 'Moscow Mule' became fashionable on the trend-setting west-coast, and soon vodka mixes spread across the country. It took a decade for vodka to get anything like a similar hold in Britain, where vodka is usually a pure spirit carefully filtered through a special form of charcoal. Its main merit is that it adds zest to whatever it is mixed with without giving any additional taste. By its purity it is held by some to be less productive of hang-overs than other spirits.

Vodka can be used for nearly all drinks traditionally based on gin.

### Vodka-based cocktails

**Vodkatini**
As for Dry Martini but increase amount of dry vermouth and immerse lemon peel (or use grapefruit rind for a change).

**Bloody Mary**
Start with 2 vodka 'on the rocks', add tomato juice; Tabasco; cayenne pepper; celery salt; Worcestershire sauce – and anything else you care to. Stir.

**Bullshot**
Can of condensed consommé; 2 vodka; celery salt, and continue as for Bloody Mary. Stir well. Strain.

**Bloody Bullshot**
Combination of the two cocktails above.

**Screwdriver**
Equal amounts vodka and iced orange juice.

**Harvey Wallbanger**
The above, plus Galliano liqueur.

**Black Russian**
Half-and-half vodka and Kahlua liqueur 'on the rocks'.

# RUM

It is not known whence comes this rum word: it could be from 'rumbustious' which once meant strong liquor, or from the Latin *saccahrum* (sugar), from a corruption of the Spanish *Ron* or the French *Rhum,* or even from the Devonian dialect 'Rumbullion'. Under English law, it is defined as a spirit distilled from sugar cane in sugar-producing countries. Rum is widely produced through the world, including the West Indies. In early times Rum was a crude spirit for fortifying slaves and it earned such nicknames as 'kill devil'. Not till the early 1700s did it gain any repute. Whilst some special rums are produced in pot-stills, the main production is now by patent distillation on a very large scale.

The alcoholic wash from the rum, made by adding water to molasses (by-product in the manufacture of cane sugar) which ferments rapidly, is then distilled. The spirit that comes from the stills is colourless and may be more or less highly flavoured, since patent distillation gives wide latitude of control in this matter. Heavy dark rums – except for de luxe qualities produced by pot-stills – have added to them a concentrated, and highly refined and coloured, sugar distillate.

*Daiquiri* *Trinity* *Manhatten* *Bloody Mary* *Atholl Brose*

Rum must be matured in wood for a minimum of three years for the British market.

Currently, light, white rum is rapidly growing in popularity.

### Rum-based cocktails

**Daiquiri**
1 white rum; ½ each fresh lemon; (lime if available) and grenadine. Shake. Strain. Serve very cold.

**Cuba Libre**
White rum 'on the rocks' in tall glass. Top with cola (some fresh lemon juice optional).

# BRANDY

Brandy certainly derives from the Dutch *brandewijn* (burnt wine): 'burning' was once a word indicating distilling. The word covers a lot of spirits, from various bases. 'Grape brandy' covers matured distillation of wine; it can come from many countries. But it is to France that we primarily look when thinking in terms of quality brandy. Many experts rate Armagnac very highly: it is a single distillation and needs specially long ageing in wood. Production is about a quarter that of cognac and here we come to the brandy that most people automatically think of when the word is used.

Cognac brandy as we understand it came into being in the seventeenth century when second distillation (to capture the 'soul of the wine') started. For centuries the fresh white wines of the Chartente area – once a proud possession of the English throne – had been exported. As early as the fifteenth century a primitive form of low-strength distilling was used to concentrate these wines and preserve them.

The white wine from which cognac comes is not good wine: it is harsh and strong. But it makes the finest brandy. As soon as the wine is made in the autumn, distilling may commence. Pot-stills of no great size are used, the type being closely regulated. The first distillation produces the *brouilli* (rather under 30% alcohol). This is re-distilled (the *bonne chauffe*) and becomes cognac. It must not contain above 72% alcohol, and this means that plenty of flavour is carried over from the wine.

Cognac is matured in oak casks in ground-floor stores called *chais*. Loss by evaporation, the 'angel's share', runs at an average 3% a year. At the annual stock-taking, casks are topped up with brandy from slightly newer casks, thus building up average age. In the instance of very fine cognac, when an average cask age of about fifty years has been achieved, the cognac will no longer improve. This exceptional spirit is then transferred to glass containers and it can then be kept indefinitely; small quantities will be added to the finest cognac blends sold by that particular house to improve the quality even further. (There is no such thing as 'vintage brandy' except for the now unusual instance where spirit is shipped a year after the vintage to mature in the importing country; in which case it may carry a year – that of the vintage. Nor does true Napoleon cognac exist, except for rare collector's items.)

Cognac is a closely protected word and may only be applied to brandy made in a well defined area centring on the town of the same name. The cognac region is subdivided into the Grande Champagne, the most prestigious, the Petite Champagne, and five bigger and less important districts. Fine champagne is not a topographical designation but a legal description of cognac brandy distilled from the produce of the Grande and Petite Champagnes only, with not less then 50% from the former.

Quality 'Three Star' brandies, some having brand-names instead of stars, will be about 5 years old on average. A usual description of 'liqueur' cognac is VSOP (Very Special Old Pale, or Superior), and above that most proprietors use various special names, plus accurate descriptions, like fine champagne, for special grades.

Superior grades of cognac are obviously only to be savoured neat. They are not for:

### Brandy-based cocktails

**Alexander**
1 each cognac; fresh cream; Crème de cacao. Shake. Strain.

**Sidecar**
1 cognac; ½ each lemon juice and cointreau. Shake. Strain.

**Champagne Cocktail**
In goblet place lump of sugar with 2 dashes angostura bitters; 1 cognac; top with iced dry champagne and serve immediately to your guests.

# APPETIZERS

If sherry makes you drowsy, and whisky does not appeal to you, try some of the other appetizers which are light in texture and not too intoxicating. They make an excellent prelude to a meal or for the first drink at a party because their delicate flavour doesn't overwhelm the taste-buds.

If on the other hand you need a pick-me-up, go for one of the anis or aquavit spirits.

### Vermouths

Vermouth is an extremely popular drink and is most commonly taken straight and sweet, on and off the rocks, or as a mainstay to many cocktails.

'French' vermouth is dry and white, and 'Italian' sweet and red, but the words have no specific geographical significance, because other wine-producing countries make both kinds.

Vermouth is blended according to strictly guarded formulae, but is basically wine infused with a variety of herbs and spices, and usually fortified with brandy. Its origins are believed to date back to the fifth century BC: they may have been evolved in Ancient Greece by Hippocrates. The oldest known commercial producer is Carpano, who began producing his vermouth in the eighteenth century, and the family is still going strong today. The word is believed to derive from the German *wermutwein*, the name for a highly-esteemed medicine, consisting of wine and wormwood.

There is a wide variety of brands available today, so it is best to try the all and then – since flavours differ quite considerably – choose the one most suited to your palate.

**Cinzano**
Cinzano, with Martini and Rossi, is probably the most widely known brand name. The company is based in Turin, and in addition to the famous Bianco, also produces a world-renowned red.

Half-and-half Cinzano Bianco and soda in a tall glass with a twist of lemon and lots of ice, makes a light, refreshing drink.

For a more decorative look, fill a glass with cracked ice, add red vermouth a few dashes of curaçao, a teaspoon of sugar and stir. Add fruit, a sprig of mint and a couple of straws.

**Chambery**
Chambery is probably the least known vermouth, but it is quite outstanding –

light, clear and fresh. Like many good things, it isn't easy to obtain, but certain specialist wine stores do stock it. It comes from the Savoy Alps of France, and is a registered trade name. Of the four producers, the oldest is Dolin, founded in 1821, the producer, too, of Chamberyzette, a delicate dry vermouth, flavoured with the juice of wild strawberries. (Another name to look for is gaudin). Like all vermouths, it is best served well-chilled and will mix happily with gin, in whatever glass you care to choose. Other branded vermouths to try are Dubonnet, St. Raphael and Lillet. Vermouths may be served however you enjoy them most, but are probably at their best in tall glasses, with lots of ice and a long twist of lemon peel. Add soda for a longer drink, or vodka for extra verve.

**Punt e Mes**

Punt e Mes is a deluxe vermouth from Carpano of Turin. It has a distinctive bitter-sweet taste, and is best served with ice and a slice of lemon in a long glass, although it goes well with gin or soda. Its taste is clean and positive, and if you drink two or three, you won't feel drowsy after lunch.

## Bitters

**Campari**

Campari has rocketed in popularity quite recently. It is a bitters, not a vermouth and with a British proof of 45° (US 50°) is classified by Customs and Excise as a spirit. It has a bitter-sweet taste, described aptly in advertisements as cryptic, is a rich pink in colour, and has a delicate bouquet.

It is made by macerating herbs in fortified wine, and is best served with ice and soda and a slice of orange. (The Italians serve it in 'one drink' Campari-soda bottles, available in any cafe or restaurant). If you like a really sharp flavour, try Campari with tonic – and insist on orange, not lemon. Half-and-half Campari and fresh orange juice – very cold – is delicious too.

**Angostura bitters**

It is worth mentioning angostura bitters just briefly here. It is good in gin and

water, and a few drops added to the water in your ice-cube tray will give the cubes a subtle fragrance that won't harm your Dry Martini in the least.

## Stronger aperitifs and spirits

The next group of drinks are considerably more emphatic, and guaranteed to work on a drooping spirit like a powerful charm.

### Anis

Anis is the general name for a wide variety of pastis, the aniseed- and liquorice-flavoured spirits, commonly associated with Marseilles.

Pernod is a soothing, subtle and exciting drink. It has many cousins all over the world with more or less the same qualities including, for example:

Ouzo in Greece, Ojen in Spain, and some types of arrack. Pernod and Pastis are a sharp, clear yellow, the colour of lemonade powder, Ouzo is clear and colourless, and they all turn a milky white when cold water is added (about one part of Pernod, for example, to five parts water). A drink best taken from a long glass.

### Tequila

The traditional spirit of Mexico, tequila is distilled from the fermented sap of the maguey, a cactus-type vegetable. The end-product is called mezcal – a firewater reputed to have hallucinatory side-effects. Tequila is a refined version of mezcal. The traditional way to drink it is with salt on the back of the hand, and a squeeze of fresh lemon juice.

### Aquavit

This is derived from the Latin *aqua vitae*, the term for distilled alcohol, and it applies to most Scandinavian spirits, flavoured or plain. They are best drunk with salt fish or the traditional smorgasbord, but they go well with German food too.

They are variously flavoured with fruit, except for Aalborg, which is clear and has a faint hint of caraway seeds.

The way to drink aquavit is very, very cold, in small glasses, and swallowed in one quick gulp.

### Slivovitz

This comes into the same category as aquavit. It is drunk widely in Central Europe and the Balkans, but is chiefly associated with Yugoslavia. It is basically plum brandy, and – a word of warning – its quality is very variable.

*Cointreau* *Crème de Cacao*

*Green Chartreuse* *Blue Curacao* *Van der Hum* *Southern comfort*

# LIQUEURS

These are alcoholic flavoured and usually sweetened, or sometimes distilled from fruit or nuts. Liqueurs are usually drunk straight after a meal.

**Advocaat (Holland).** Brandy, eggs and vanilla. Sweet and widely popular.

**Anisette (France).** Colourless, aniseed flavoured. Similar in taste to Goldwasser from Germany, which is laced with particles of gold leaf.

**Apricot Brandy (many countries).** Speaks for itself. Sweet.

**Aquavit (Denmark).** Colourless grain or potato spirit, flavoured with caraway seeds. Very potent and fiery. Usually tossed down at a gulp before a meal. Good for combatting long Scandinavian winters.

**Benedictine (France).** Probably the oldest and still one of the best liqueurs. First distilled by the Benedictine monks in the early sixteenth century as a medicine for malaria – and a tonic to revive tired clergy. Flavouring includes arnica, hyssop, vanilla, cinnamon, coriander, nutmeg, mace, saffron and cardamom.

**Calvados (France).** Apple brandy from Normandy. Sold at six years old or over – making it superior to the American Applejack.

**Crème de Cassis (France).** Very sweet and blackcurranty. Often confused with the non-alcoholic cordial called Sirop de Cassis.

**Chartreuse (France).** Made by Carthusian monks near Grenoble. Comes in two colours – green and yellow. The latter is less potent and much sweeter.

**Cherry brandy (many countries).** Speaks for itself. Very sweet.

**Cointreau (France).** Colourless, orange-flavoured liqueur, similar to Grand Marnier.

**Crème de Cacao (France).** Very sweet, tasting strongly of chocolate. Made from cocoa beans.

**Crème de Menthe (France).** Strongly peppermint-flavoured. Usually drunk well iced.

**Curacao (West Indies).** Similar to Cointreau. The colour is either golden or a delicate blue.

**Drambuie (Scotland).** Whisky, honey and herbs. The recipe is said to have been a gift to an ancestor of the present proprietors from that noted drinker, Bonnie Prince Charlie.

**Forbidden Fruit (America).** Orange and honey flavoured, with a brandy base. The colour is a beautiful golden brown.

**Framboise (France).** Colourless, dry, and distilled from raspberries. Delicious served chilled or otherwise.

*Calvados* *Cherry brandy*

*Crème de Cassis* *Kahlua* *Strega*

**Galliano (Italy).** Pale yellow. Somewhat similar in flavour to Strega.
**Grand Marnier** (see Cointreau).
**Grappa** (see Marc).
**Kirsch (Germany).** Colourless. Distilled from the juice and kernels of German cherries. Extra dry and good. Maraschino is similar but sweet.
**Kahlua (Mexico).** Like Creme de Cacao, made with cocoa beans and grain spirit. Popular in the USA and delicious poured over ice-cream.
**Kümmel (Baltic States).** Vodka and caraway seeds. Fine if you like caraway seeds.
**Marc (France).** Made from the pressing of skins, pips and stems of grapes of the burgundy and champagne districts which have already been pressed to make wine. Similar to Grappa (Italy).
**Mirabelle (France).** Plum brandy from golden-yellow plums. Resembles slivovitz (Yugoslavia), but without the latter's fiery quality.
**Sloe's Gin (Britain).** Sugar, sloes and gin, and very good indeed, especially for people who don't drink but who need something sweet to hold at parties and festivities.
**Southern Comfort (USA).** Made from bourbon and peaches, presumably to console the South for defeat in the American Civil War.
**Strega (Italy).** Said to be flavoured with aromatic herbs and barks, but some people claim that it's more like very sweet varnish!
**Tia Maria (Jamaica).** Rum flavoured with coffee beans. It will transform the dullest vanilla ice-cream into a real treat.
**Van der Hum (South Africa).** The colour is russet brown and the flavour a rich tangerine.

***Above** Punch is an ideal drink to serve during the Christmas festivities – and will bring joy to everyone.*

# HOT'N PUNCHY

Breaking the ice can have more than a social meaning. There are those days and nights when frost and snow make a hot drink the best welcome and the best stirrup-cup for the departing guest.

### Mulls, toddies and others

There's a long list of party drinks that can be hot. Punches, possets, mulls, toddies and grogs – all good warmer-uppers, even their names sing a happy party song. And, besides providing fun in the making as well as in the drinking, they can be comparatively easy on the purse. Obviously since they are mixed drinks, deriving their character from sugar, spices and other non-wine ingredients, it would be folly to use fine wines for them. Where a recipe says claret or burgundy, any of the most bourgeois growths will be quite satisfactory – or, indeed, any wine of similar style from another country, whether it is a branded wine or not.

But do try them out first. For that matter, since most of these drinks specify sugar, spices and other ingredients 'to taste', they're all worthy of a little rehearsal before the party – say, with your family or a few friends. It isn't a painful exercise. Another important point is that since the drinks are hot, they're best served in goblets or other containers which have handles. Silver or pewter may be considered status symbols but, in fact, metal cups conduct heat and may be a hazard to tender lips, so little china or glass mugs are better. If they're glass and your toddy is really hot – which is the object of the exercise – a spoon placed in the cup during the pouring will dissipate the heat and save breakages and nasty accidents.

One other point: mulls, punches and the like used to be warmed by plunging a red-hot poker in them. Nowadays it's much more efficient to heat them gently on the stove. Get them hot but never let them boil unless you want to drive off all the benign influence of the alcohol – which you don't, presumably, or you wouldn't be reading this.

### Punches

Let's take punches, for instance. In the eighteenth century the making of punch was a high-society ritual, undertaken with flourish and solemnity. The bewigged host, standing at the head of his table, had the undivided attention of his guests as they watched him summon servant after servant to bring each successive ingredient to go into the punch bowl.

Punch is still fun. To begin with, it's a natural starter for general conversation. Does the word 'punch' come from the Hindustani panch (meaning five), since the ingredients when it was first introduced from India in the seventeenth century were five – spirit, fruit juice, water, spices and sugar? But weren't some of the original recipes of only three ingredients and some of them of six ingredients? And anyhow, isn't it simpler to take the word simply to be an abbreviation of 'puncheon', the name of the casks from which the sailors on the East India run drew their grog rations? "But," says your favourite extrovert guest, "does all this matter – when your punch is the greatest?" If he is being truthful, the heart of your successful punch will still be those five ingredients, though the proportions can be infinitely varied, according to your guests, to their tastes and capacities – and to yours too. As to quantities for a party, a couple of 125ml/5 fl oz punch goblets are enough for some, too much for others. It is up to you to know the inexperienced drinkers, who can be quietly given a bit more hot water and fruit juice, and the rather more experienced ones, who take your standard-mixture punch. Again, it's worth some rehearsal. Here's a warmer-upper which truly began in the eighteenth century and is sometimes called Dr. Johnson's Choice. It makes about 12 to 15 punch glasses or goblets.

### Dr. Johnson

Heat two bottles of claret gently with one sliced orange, 12 lumps of sugar which have been rubbed on the orange rind, and six cloves. Bring the mixture nearly to the boil and remove it from the stove, immediately adding a wine glassful (about 150 ml/6 fl oz) of one of the orange liqueurs (branded cointreau, Grand Marnier, South Africa's Van der Hum or simply Curacao) and the same quantity of brandy. Ladle it into your punch cups and sprinkle each with nutmeg.

***Below*** *Festive, spicy and warming, a red wine mull is the perfect drink to serve at a winter party.*

### The Bishop

For 12 to 15 drinks, stud a lemon with cloves and bake it in a moderate oven for 30 minutes. Heat 1 L/40 fl oz of port to just below simmering point. In another pan boil 500 ml/20 fl oz water with 1 teaspoonful mixed spices and add it to the hot port with the baked lemon. Rub 50 g/2 oz lump sugar into the rind of another lemon and put this sugar into the punch bowl with the juice of ½ lemon and pour in the hot wine.

## Fruit juice specials

### Home-made lemonade

Nice to serve this from a tall glass jug, with a float of lemon, lime, cucumber slices, or a sprig of mint. This recipe makes about 1 L/40 fl oz. Wash 3 lemons cut them in halves and squeeze the juice. Pare off the rind very thinly and put it with 100-150 g/4-6 oz of castor [fine] sugar into a basin. Add 750 ml/30 fl oz of boiling water, cover and leave until cold, stirring occasionally. Strain the lemon juice, and chill well before serving.

### Orangeade

This is made by the same method as the lemonade, but in the proportions of 2 oranges and 1 lemon, 50 g/2 oz of castor [fine] sugar and 500 ml/2 fl oz of boiling water.

### Strawberry crush

A year-round favourite for sweet-tooths. For about 5 servings, in stemmed goblets, put 350 g/¾ lb of washed and hulled strawberries with 250 ml/10 fl oz of orange juice and sugar syrup to taste, into an electric blender, to make a purée. Without a blender, just sieve the strawberries, then mix them with the orange juice and the sugar syrup. Mix equal parts of the strawberry crush with crushed ice in goblets (or tumblers) and serve at once. Suck through straws or use long spoons. A variation: If fresh limes are available, substitute them for the orange. Or use sieved raspberries instead of strawberries.

### Tomato special

The easiest way is to buy your favourite tomato juice, and spice it up a bit. It must be chilled, otherwise it is cloying to the palate. A little goes a long way. If you want to make you own chilled tomato appetizers, use Italian canned tomatoes. Blend and sieve them. Chill thoroughly. Add to taste salt, freshly milled black pepper, and either Worcestershire sauce or Tabasco. Chill again. Don't dilute with ice. If you happen to have some fresh basil, finely chopped, as a garnish, you will win friends and create a talking point. Otherwise add lemon floats to the chilled jug from which you're serving.

### Spice island punch

For 10-15 glasses mix together 750 ml/30 fl oz of fresh orange juice, 250 ml/10 fl oz of canned pineapple juice, the juice and pared rind of 1 lemon, ½ level teaspoon each of grated nutmeg and mixed spice and 6 cloves in a big jug. Strain, chill well, and add 1 L/40 fl oz of ginger ale, putting crushed ice into individual glasses just before serving to your family and friends.

# COFFEE-PLUS A DASH

No-one who has ever woken up in Paris to smell the aroma of the morning's coffee rising from the courtyard of the hotel is ever likely to forget it. In the same way, a fine cup of coffee after a drinks, buffet party or any social gathering rates as a first class drink if properly made. But too often, it turns out to be bitter and insipid. Here's how to make it well, and how to add a dash of something stronger.

### Method of making

First of all, coffee must be properly made. The usual methods, in a variety of machinery, are straining, percolating and filtering. Putting coffee in a pot, adding boiling water and straining the resulting infusion is the most popular but disperses all the aroma. Further, any instrument or device made of metal or glass which is elaborate and difficult to work should be given away. Buy paper filters and a cone. Have your coffee ground to the right degree – very fine if you have your own grinder. Put 35 g/1¼ oz per 500 ml/20 fl oz in the cone, filter sitting on a pot that's warming on the stove. Pour in boiling water, measured in a cup. Repeat until the correct number of cupfuls is in the bottom of the pot. The virtue of the paper filter is that the coffee is not itself boiled and acid ingredients are held back. It can even be successfully re-heated but NOT boiled.

The alternative method is to use a coffee-pot with a plunger. This works on almost the same principle as the filter. Put in 35 g/1¼ oz per 500 ml/20 fl oz of water. Pour on the boiling water. Stir. Let the coffee stand for three to five minutes. Depress the plunger and the coffee is made.

If you suffer from hard water, a water softener would improve out of recognition not only your coffee but also cooking generally (and bathing!). The next hurdle is the choice of coffee.

### The coffee to choose

In Europe the habit is to roast the beans more than is popular in Britain or America – hence the darker colour of the

*Left Fruit punches are a good idea to serve at a party for teetotallers.*

'continental' coffees. Experiment with various fresh-roasted coffees until you find the one that suits you – and your water supply – best. Breakfast coffee sometimes doesn't go well after dinner, so have two kinds in store. Buy as little at a time as is practical: large amounts of ground coffee go stale very quickly. For dinner try Blue Mountain from Jamaica or Chagga from the volcanic lower slopes of Mount Meru. Ever since the day, so the story goes, when an Arab goatherd in the Yemen noticed that his goats perked up after eating the red berries of wild coffee, people have been overdoing the drinking of coffee at night, perking themselves up just before going to bed. The coffee is wrongly blamed for insomnia; moderation is the cure.

## Turkish coffee

Since coffee succeeded where Turkish troops failed to penetrate Western Europe, it is worth considering how the Turkish soldiers prepared it at home – particularly since the pulverized ingredient they used is now fairly easy to obtain. This can be either in a copper Turkish copper pot, known as an Ibrik, or in a saucepan. Use pulverized coffee, obtainable from specialist coffee shops. For four people pour a standard cup and a half of water into a pan with six teaspoonsful of castor [fine] sugar. Bring to boiling point. Add three heaped dessertspoonsful of very finely ground coffee. Bring to the boil three times. Take pan off the heat and add a few drops of cold water. With a spoon take a little of the froth from the surface of the coffee and put into each small coffee cup. Pour the coffee very slowly into the cup.

*Below Made with strong black coffee, sugar, cream and ice-cream, iced coffee is an unusual, refreshing drink to serve at the end of your party.*

## Coffee plus alcohol

The popularity of coffee among the Moslem Turks and Arabs was as a substitute for alcohol, forbidden them by religion. In Christian countries, where no such prohibition exists, the invogorating properties of coffee are enhanced by the addition of alcohol. In Italy a slug of aniseed (anis, anice) ensures a pleasant wakefulness for the business of the later evening.

Call it Highland coffee if you lace it with a good dollop of a single-malt whisky or Drambuie, café royal if you add cognac. Carribean coffee with a fine Barbados rum, Danish with aquavit, Mexican with kahlua, bourbon with Southern comfort, Russian with vodka, Normandy with calvados, or witch's coffee with strega.

In Ireland and elsewhere the most renowned and recent coffee/alcohol invention, Gaelic (or Irish) coffee, has a world wide reputation. Here is the recipe:

## Gaelic (or Irish) coffee

Heat a stemmed whiskey glass. Pour in a good slug of Irish whiskey. Add three cubes of sugar. Fill glass with strong black coffee to within one inch of the brim and stir to dissolve sugar. Top to brim of glass with double cream poured carefully over the back of a spoon so that it floats on top of the coffee. Do not stir as the best flavour is obtained by drinking the coffee and whiskey through the cream.

## Spiced coffee

Spiced coffee is rather a showy affair, and is flamed in a silver bowl or chafing dish called variously brule, brulot or diable. You need a bowl over a spirit lamp or candle warmer. For 12 to 15 coffee cups, use a bottle of brandy and 1½ pints of strong coffee. Into the bowl put the thinly pared rind of an orange, 4 large sugar lumps well rubbed with lemon rind to absorb the zest, 4 cloves, 2.5 cm [1 in] of stick cinnamon, 2.5 cm [1 in] of vanilla pod and the brandy. With a long-handled ladle, lift out some of the warmed brandy, set it alight and lower it into the bowl to set the mixture alight. Pour in the hot coffee gently, raising the liquid a ladleful at a time to mix everything until the flames die. While the applause for the spectacular display goes on, ladle the mixture into the coffee cups of your appreciative guests.

## Iced coffee

A simple, easy to prepare drink, iced coffee is delicious. You will need castor [fine] sugar, a small carton of single [light] cream, a small block of vanilla ice-cream and coffee. Use only coffee made from fresh coffee beans.

Pour about 750 ml/1½ pts/3¾ cups of freshly made hot coffee into a medium-sized mixing bowl. Stir in some sugar and set aside to cool. The amount of sugar added is a matter of personal taste.

Using a wire whisk or a rotary beater, beat the cream and ice-cream into the coffee. Continue beating until smoothe and frothy.

Pour the coffee mixture into a jug and chill in the refrigerator, stirring occasionally.

Serve with ice cubes.

# AFTER THE PARTY'S OVER

Even the wisest of us sometimes wish we hadn't had quite so many, or such varied, drinks the night before.

### What causes hang-over?

Quite simply, hang-overs are caused by too much. Of course, one man's excess may be another's aperitif, and even your own vulnerability may vary from day to day, depending on how well or tired you are, and whether the poor system is being strained in some other way – through over-eating or too much smoking. Basically it's a kind of poisoning – the system gets flooded with alcohol and can't get rid of it quickly enough. The question is are there any real remedies for this lugubrious condition?

### Food before

It's always wise to eat well before spending an evening drinking. It gives the lining of the stomach a buffer against the onslaught of alcohol.

### Dangerous drinks

Some drinks are more likely to produce a hang-over in some people than others – for example, red wine, rum, whisky and, most lethal of all, brandy. On the other hand, you're more likely to wake up feeling fresh and happy after drinking white wine, gin or vodka. The operative word is OR. Mixing wines and spirits is liable to lead to trouble too. Beware also of too much cheap champagne, cheap sour wine, and unidentified fruit cups!

### Water

The best answer of course, is to drink lots and lots of water on getting home from the party and before going to bed, with or without some fizzy additive. Plenty of water will do more for the pain than anything else as alcohol is very dehydrating and the dehydration is a prime cause of headaches. If you forgot to drink a lot of water just before you went to bed, drink much more water than you feel you actually want when you wake

### Cigarettes

Half the trouble with many parties is the quantity of smoke which creates a heavy, thick atmosphere guaranteed to produce headaches. Cigarette smoking aggravates the effects of drinking too.

### Kaolin and morphine mixture

If someone is feeling distinctly queasy, he should pop into a chemist or drugstore and down a dose of kaolin and morphine mixture. It settles the stomach miraculously and stops the boat rocking.

### Patent cures

Fernet Branca is an Italian bitters which certainly lives up to that description. Perhaps it's the shock of the flavour or the soothing properties of the herbs but either way, some people find it curative. Underberg is a German cure – very alcoholic and very effective.

### Curative recipes

These are really designed for people who are longing for a reviving sip of alcohol but realise it should be tempered with a good, nutritional base. Prairie Oyster is a mixture of 25 g/1 oz brandy, 1 teaspoon wine vinegar, 1 teaspoon Worcestershire sauce, a dash cayenne pepper and 1 egg yolk.

Pour the first four ingredients over the egg and swallow – if possible – without breaking the egg!

Both a Bloody Mary and a Bull Shot give a good cushion of tomato juice or consommé.

### Oxygen

Medical students swear by a whiff of oxygen. A few deep breaths at an open window or a brisk walk are helpful for anyone without a cylinder to hand. Some sufferers find that in mountainous country a journey up the ski-lift above 5,000 feet will work wonders.

### Food after

The morning after – and if you can bear it, chew but don't swallow an orange or a lemon to clean out the bottom of the birdcage. It's vital not to swallow the fruit: there's enough acid already in your stomach.

Breakfast should consist of porridge (to reline the stomach), and then kippers, for protein and salt to replace the minerals washed away by the alcohol (their absence can give you cramp). The Russians, with a wisdom learned from centuries of suffering under the effects of rough vodka and tyranny, hand round salt fish and bread with salt on it to counter desalination while drinking.

# DRINKS PARTY

## FINGER FOODS

### Egg and caviar on black bread

Egg and caviar on rye bread makes a delicious but unusual tidbit for a drinks party.

MAKES 32

**6 eggs**
**8 slices of rye bread**
**50 g/2 oz/4 tablespoons butter**
**6 tablespoons mayonnaise**
**100 g/4 oz Danish caviar [lumpfish roe]**

TO GARNISH

**Sprigs of parsley**

Hard boil the eggs and cool. Remove the shells and thinly slice the eggs.

Cut four round shapes from each slice of rye bread, to make 32 shapes.

Spread with butter and place a slice of egg on each one. Place a small amount of mayonnaise in the middle of the egg and carefully put half a teaspoon of the caviar on top of each.

Garnish with small sprigs of parsley.

### Cheese sputniks

Cheese sputniks make excellent tidbits for a drinks party. Instead of an orange use a fresh pineapple, or a red or white cabbage.

20 SERVINGS

**4 large oranges**
**675 g/1½ lb mild cheese**
**25 large black grapes**
**120 wooden cocktail sticks**
**25 stuffed green olives**
**25 walnut halves**
**150 g/6 oz canned pineapple cubes**
**150 g/6 oz canned mandarin oranges**

Cut a thin slice from the base of the oranges to enable them to stand up.

Cut the cheese in 1.3 cm [½ in] cubes and divide them into four piles.

Place a black grape on top of a cheese cube and gently pierce both with a cocktail stick. Stick this into one of the oranges, leaving enough showing so that people can remove it easily. Follow the same procedure with an olive on top of the cheese, then a walnut, a pineapple cube, a mandarin segment and so on until the oranges are thickly covered.

*Left Cheese sputniks make excellent party snacks. Make up your own varieties as well as the ones given.*

*Above Devils and angels on horseback are always popular at parties so be sure to make plenty. Try other fillings too.*

### Devils on horseback

These bacon rolls stuffed with prunes are delicious appetizers. For a variation make angels on horseback. Use fresh or smoked oysters instead of the stuffed prunes, and cook as before.

8 SERVINGS

**16 large prunes**
**8 strips of bacon**
**8 anchovy fillets**
**16 blanched almonds**
**16 wooden cocktail sticks**

Soak the prunes overnight in tea. Heat oven to Gas Mark 7, 200°C [400°F].

Simmer the prunes until tender, for 10-15 minutes. Drain, and when they are cool carefully remove the stones.

Remove the rind from the bacon and cut each strip in half. Flatten on a chopping board.

Cut the anchovy fillets in half and wrap each half around a blanched almond. Place this inside a prune and wrap the bacon piece around the stuffed prune. Secure each with a cocktail stick, place on a baking tray and cook for 10-12 minutes.

### Smoked salmon and dill rolls

Smoked salmon rolls are a guaranteed success for any drinks party.

MAKES 16-20 ROLLS

**4 large slices of smoked salmon**
**200 ml/8 fl oz/1 cup double [heavy] cream**
**dried dill weed**
**freshly ground black pepper**
**juice of 1 lemon**
**20 wooden cocktail sticks**

Stiffly beat the cream and add the dill weed to taste. Spread on to the smoked salmon slices, and sprinkle with pepper. Roll each slice up tightly and wrap in greaseproof or waxed paper. Place in the refrigerator for at least one hour before cutting into pieces.

Pierce each piece with a cocktail stick, and squeeze a little lemon juice over them.

## Ham and cream cheese rolls

The two different textures of ham and cream cheese combine to make an appetizing nibble.

MAKES 16-20 ROLLS

**4 large slices of lean ham**
**150 g/6 oz cream cheese**
**4 tablespoons chopped fresh chives**
**20 wooden cocktail sticks**

Spread the ham with the cream cheese, sprinkle with chopped chives and roll up very tightly. Cut into pieces and secure each by piercing it with a cocktail stick.

## Sausages in chutney sauce

Sausages in chutney sauce make an interesting change from plain sausages on sticks.

16 SERVINGS

**1 kg/2 lb small pork sausages**
**100 g/4 oz/1 scant cup chopped almonds**
**100 ml/4 fl oz/½ cup chutney sauce**

Heat oven to Gas Mark 5, 190°C [375°F]. Twist each sausage in half and cut at the new join, using kitchen scissors. Bake for 20 minutes.

Strain off the fat, transfer to a serving dish, and put the chutney sauce carefully over them.

Sprinkle with the chopped almonds and serve with cocktail sticks.

## Beef and horseradish rolls

Sliced cooked beef wrapped round horse radish sauce makes a palatable savoury on a stick.

MAKES 16 ROLLS

**4 slices of medium rare cooked beef**
**100 ml/4 fl oz/½ cup double [heavy] cream**
**2 tablespoons horseradish sauce**
**16 wooden cocktail sticks**

Whip the cream until stiff, and mix with the horseradish sauce. Spread on to the slices of beef, roll up, cut into pieces and serve each piece pierced with a cocktail stick.

## Cheese-stuffed celery

Crisp and crunchy celery filled with a cream cheese mixture makes an unusual tidbit.

MAKES 50

**10 celery stalks**
**300 g/12 oz cream cheese**
**3 tablespoons chives, finely chopped**
**4 drops Tabasco**
**salt and pepper**

Wash the celery, discard the leaves and cut into 5 cm [2 in] pieces.

Mix the cheese with the chives and Tabasco. Season with a little salt and pepper.

Using a piping bag with a fluted nozzle pipe the cheese into the hollow of the celery pieces.

## Pizza toast

Hot bite-sized mock pizzas will be eagerly eaten when served at a drinks or cocktail party.

8 SERVINGS

**8 slices of white bread**
**25 g/1 oz/2 tablespoons butter**
**1 small onion, finely chopped**
**1 tablespoon olive oil**
**2 tablespoons tomato purée [paste]**
**8 large black olives**
**4 anchovy fillets, finely chopped**
**½ teaspoon basil, dried**
**100 g/4 oz/1 cup grated gruyère [Swiss] cheese**

Heat the grill [broiler].

Cut the crusts from the slices of bread and cut the slices in half. Fry in the butter until golden but not brown. Drain on absorbent kitchen paper.

Finely chop the onion and fry in the oil until soft, add the tomato purée [paste] and cook for another minute. Place in a small mixing bowl.

Stone the black olives and chop the flesh. Add them to the onion mixture. Finely chop the anchovy fillets and mix with the rest.

Add the tomato and the basil and mix well.

Spread the mixture on the fried bread, sprinkle with the grated cheese and place under a hot grill [broiler] for 5-7 minutes.

Serve your pizza toast sizzling hot to get the best results.

## Tuna fish pâté

Tuna fish pâté makes a tasty hors d'oeuvre served with toast.

8 SERVINGS

**200 g/8 oz canned tuna fish**
**150 g/6 oz/¾ cup butter**
**2 tablespoons lemon juice**
**2 tablespoons olive oil**
**2 tablespoons brandy**
**1 garlic clove, crushed**
**1 tablespoon chopped parsley**
**1 medium-sized onion, peeled and grated**
**salt and pepper**

Drain the tuna fish and melt the butter.

Mash the tuna fish with the lemon juice, olive oil and brandy. Add the melted butter, garlic, parsley, grated onion and seasoning. Beat until smooth, or put in an electric blender.

Adjust the seasoning and refrigerate until required.

Serve with hot toast.

## Salami on black bread

Highly seasoned, dry sausage on rye bread makes a tasty appetizer to serve.

8 SERVINGS

**4 slices dark rye bread**
**25 g/1 oz/2 tablespoons butter**
**8 lettuce leaves**
**2 medium-sized onions**
**24 slices salami, thinly cut**
**8 parsley sprigs**

Cut the slices of rye bread into halves and butter them. Place a lettuce leaf on top of each slice.

Thinly slice the onions and push into rings.

Fold the salami slices loosely in half and arrange 3 slices on each slice of bread.

Garnish with sprigs of parsley and the smallest of the onions rings.

## Cheese aigrettes

Bite-sized cheese snacks are delicious served piping hot.

8 SERVINGS

**75 g/3 oz/6 tablespoons butter**
**200 ml/8 fl oz/1 cup stock made up from ½ chicken stock cube**
**125 g/5 oz/1¼ cups flour, sifted**
**4 eggs, beaten**
**50 g/2 oz/½ cup gruyère [Swiss] cheese, grated**
**50 g/2 oz/½ cup Parmesan cheese, grated**
**pinch cayenne pepper**

*Above Cheese aigrèttes are delightfully unusual nibbles for a drinks party*

**½ teaspoon dry mustard**
**salt and pepper**
**oil for frying**

Heat oven to Gas Mark 2, 150°C [300°F].

Place the butter and the stock in a saucepan and bring to the boil. Remove the pan from the stove and tip all the flour in quickly. Beat well until the mixture is smooth and leaves the sides of the pan.

Beat the eggs gradually. The grated cheese, cayenne pepper, dry mustard and a little salt and pepper and mix well.

Heat the oil in a heavy saucepan and drop in teaspoonsful of the mixture. Fry for 7-10 minutes until golden brown.

Drain well on kitchen paper and keep warm in the oven until ready to serve.

## Gorgonzola biscuits [crackers]

Flavourful savoury biscuits [crackers] which use that fine Italian cheese, Gorgonzola, these biscuits [crackers] may be served on their own with drinks.

40 BISCUITS

**50 g/2 oz/¼ cup butter**
**150 g/6 oz Gorgonzola cheese**
**200 g/8 oz/2 cups flour, sifted**
**1 egg**
**¼ teaspoon salt**
**¼ teaspoon black pepper**
**1 tablespoon water**
**optional**

In a medium-sized mixing bowl, cream the butter with a wooden spoon until it is soft. Add the cheese and mash it into

*Below These highly flavoured Gorgonzola biscuits [crackers] make an excellent accompaniment to drinks.*

the butter. Cream well, blend in the flour, egg, salt and pepper. Knead the mixture lightly to form a smooth dough. If the dough is too dry, add the water. Cover the dough and place it in the refrigerator to chill for 30 minutes.

Preheat the oven to hot Gas Mark 7, 220°C [425°F].

On a lightly floured surface, roll out the dough into a rectangular shape 6 mm [¼ in] thick. Trim the edges of the dough and cut into 2.5 cm [1 in] squares with a sharp knife. Transfer the squares to a large baking sheet and place it in the oven. Bake the biscuits [crackers] for 12 to 15 minutes or until they are golden brown.

Remove the baking sheet from the oven and cool the biscuits [crackers] on a wire rack.

## Savoury cheese straws

These light savoury biscuits [crackers] are especially popular served with apéritifs.

**200 g/8 oz of plain flour**
**salt and cayenne pepper**
**100 g/4 oz of butter**
**75 g/3 oz of strong Cheddar cheese (grated)**
**25 g/1 oz of grated Parmesan cheese**
**2 egg yolks**
**cold water**

Heat oven to Gas Mark 6, 200°C [400°F].

Put flour into mixing bowl, with a little salt and cayenne pepper. Rub in butter until the mixture resembles fine breadcrumbs.

Mix in grated cheeses thoroughly. Add beaten egg yolks and enough cold water to make a stiff dough. Turn out onto a floured board and roll out pastry into an oblong about 37.5 cm [15 in] long and 12.5 cm [5 in] wide.

Cut into straws approximately 6.3 cm [2½ in] long and 6 mm [¼ in] wide. Twist each straw and place them on a prepared greased baking tray.

Bake for 10-15 minutes until golden-brown. Cool and store in an airtight tin. This mixture can also be used to make small cheese biscuits [crackers].

***Left*** *Top of picture is a sour cream dip. Serve with crunchy pieces of carrot and cauliflower to scoop it up with. In the centre are a variety of savoury spreads. Below are delicious savoury cheese straws.*

***Right*** *Dips served with crudités make a colourful display for a drinks or a buffet party. All are tasty as well as economical.*

# DIPS

These are always very popular at parties, are easily made, and can with very little effort be made to look extremely attractive. Almost any pâté or spread may be turned into a dip, by adding whipped cream, yoghurt, French dressing, thick mayonnaise or a soft cream cheese. The most important point to remember when making dips is to achieve a really thick consistency – for if they are at all runny, your guests as well as your carpets will be covered with messy dribbles. Serve dips with lots of small biscuits [crackers], crispbreads, potato crisps [chips] – and crudités composed of strips of raw carrot, celery sticks, raw cauliflower florets, scrubbed radishes, and anything else you can think of.

## Cream cheese and salami dip

Quick and easy to prepare, this cream cheese dip is ideal to serve with crudités for a party.

MAKES 450 G/1 LB

**1 medium-sized onion**

100 g/4 oz thinly sliced salami
200 g/8 oz cream cheese
150 ml/6 fl oz/¾ cup sour cream

Grate the onion. Cut the slices of salami into thin strips.

Mix the cream cheese with the sour cream, add the onion and the salami strips mix well and serve with potato crisps [chips].

## Sour cream dip

Serve this dip with crunchy pieces of carrot and cauliflower to scoop it up with.

6 SERVINGS

125 g/5 oz carton of soured cream
1 tablespoon of chilli sauce
(from a bottle)
1 teaspoon of dried mustard powder
1 medium onion (grated)
1 teaspoonful of Worcestershire sauce
1 tablespoon of chopped chives
½ teaspoon freshly-ground pepper
½ teaspoon of salt

Mix everything together, and chill one hour before serving.

## Avocado dip

Spicy and delicious, this dip is easily made. It is the perfect dip for a drinks party.

6 SERVINGS

1 medium-sized ripe avocado
1 tablespoon of lemon juice
125 g/5 oz carton of soured cream
1 clove of garlic (crushed)
1 medium onion (grated)
half a green pepper (chopped small)
salt, freshly-ground black pepper
2 tomatoes (chopped small)

Slice the avocado in two and remove the stone.

Scoop out all the flesh into a bowl, making sure you get all the very green flesh next to the skin (this helps to make the dip a good colour).

Thoroughly mix in the tablespoon of lemon juice, the salt and freshly-milled black pepper.

Now add the soured cream and mix till smooth, either with rotary whisk or electric beater.

Add the garlic, onion, green pepper and tomatoes. Stir, taste to check the seasoning and chill before serving. Never make this until the day you need it, as it tends to discolour if left overnight.

*Above A piquant dip, avocado dip is fabulous for a drinks party. Blend the ingredients together until smooth and thick. Serve with crudités.*

## Blue cheese dip

This strong tasting cheese dip will be much appreciated by those with a more sophisticated palate.

6 SERVINGS

100 g/¼ lb Gorgonzola cheese
125 g/5 oz carton of soured cream
1 medium onion (grated)
1 teaspoon of freshly-ground pepper

Cream the cheese by mixing with a large fork. Add the soured cream, a little at a time, until it's all in and the mixture looks creamy.

Add the grated onion and pepper. Chill in the refrigerator. Serve immediately with crudités.

## Avocado and cheese dip

Serve with julienne sticks of fresh raw vegetables, potato crisps [chips] or biscuits [crackers].

MAKES 675 G/1½ LB

**3 medium-sized avocado pears**
**3 tablespoons mayonnaise**
**4 drops Tabasco**
**2 tablespoons lemon juice**
**2 tablespoons grated onion**
**1 garlic clove, crushed**
**50 g/2 oz/½ cup strong cheese, grated**
**100 ml/4 fl oz/½ cup double [heavy] cream**
**salt and pepper**

Peel and stone the avocados. Using a wooden spoon push the avocado flesh through a strainer into a bowl, or use a food mill.

Mix in the mayonnaise, Tabasco sauce, lemon juice, grated onion, crushed garlic and grated cheese.

Beat the cream until stiff and fold into the avocado mixture.

Season with salt and pepper and then cover the bowl and refrigerate until well chilled.

## Garlic mayonnaise with raw vegetables

An appealing appetizer for a buffet or cocktail party. Serve surrounded by vegetable crudités.

8 SERVINGS

**250 ml/10 fl oz/1¼ cups aioli**
**4 celery stalks**
**4 medium-sized carrots**
**23 small spring onions [scallions]**

Make the aioli (see basic recipes).

Scrape and cut the carrots in to 1.3 cm [½ in] wide and 5 cm [2 in] long sticks. Wash and scrub the celery stalks and cut into similar pieces. Trim and wash the spring onions [scallions].

Spoon the aioli into a tall stemmed glass, and surround with neat piles of the vegetable sticks and spring onions [scallions].

## Taramasalata

This Greek hors d'oeuvre is traditionally made with tarama, the dried and pressed roe of the grey mullet, but smoked cod's roe is widely used today when tarama is not available. Serve taramasalata with pitta.

6 SERVINGS

**450 g/1 lb smoked cod's roe, skinned**
**4 slices white bread, crusts removed and soaked in milk for 15 minutes**
**4 garlic cloves, crushed**
**250 ml/10 fl oz/1¼ cups olive oil**
**4 tablespoons lemon juice**
**½ teaspoon freshly ground black pepper**
**¼ cucumber, thinly sliced**
**6 firm tomatoes, sliced**
**6 black olives**

Place the cod's roe in a large mixing bowl and pound it with the end of a rolling pin, or use a pestle and mortar, until the gritty texture is eliminated.

Squeeze as much moisture out of the bread as possible and add it to the bowl, with the garlic. Continue pounding until the mixture is smooth.

Add the oil, a few drops at a time, pounding constantly and adding a little of the lemon juice from time to time. Continue pounding until the mixture forms a soft, smooth paste and is pale pink in colour.

Alternatively, place all the ingredients in the jar of an electric blender and blend until a soft paste is formed.

Beat the pepper into the mixture and arrange equal quantities of it on 6 small serving plates. Surround the paste with cucumber and tomato slices and top each portion with an olive. Serve immediately.

*Below Taramasalata is a very popular dip for parties. Serve with pitta bread or hot crusty bread.*

## Onion dip

Serve this tasty and easy-to-make onion dip at buffet parties or as an appetizer with celery stalks, sliced green peppers, French bread or Melba toast and butter.

ABOUT 675 G/1½ LB

**450 g/1 lb cream cheese**
**4 tablespoons double [heavy] cream**
**4 tablespoons sour cream**
**1 tablespoon lemon juice**
**½ teaspoon Tabasco sauce**
**½ teaspoon prepared French mustard**
**½ teaspoon salt**
**½ teaspoon celery salt**
**½ teaspoon black pepper**
**1 tablespoon paprika**
**2 spring onions [scallions], very finely chopped**
**2 small shallots, very finely chopped**
**4 small white onions, finely chopped**
**2 tablespoons chopped fresh chives**

In a medium-sized mixing bowl, beat the cream cheese with a wooden spoon until it is soft. Beat in the cream, sour cream, lemon juice, Tabasco sauce, mustard, salt, celery salt, pepper and paprika.

Add the spring onions [scallions], shallots, onions and chives. Combine the mixture thoroughly and spoon it into a glass serving dish.

Place the dip in the refrigerator and chill it for 1 hour before serving.

## Cream cheese dip with rosemary

This dip is delicious sandwiched between two small crackers.

6 SERVINGS

**150 g/6 oz cream cheese**
**½ teaspoon powdered rosemary**
**200 ml/8 fl oz/1 cup mayonnaise**
**salt and pepper**

Mix the cream cheese well with the powdered rosemary and add the mayonnaise. Taste, and add the salt and pepper.

## Curried Cheddar dip

This unusual hot and spicy cheese dip will delight your guests.

MAKES 450 G/1 LB

**200 g/8 oz/1 cup of butter**
**2 teaspoons curry powder**
**150 g/6 oz Cheddar cheese**
**3 tablespoons mango chutney**
**50 g/2 oz/½ cup desiccated [shredded] coconut**
**125 ml/5 fl oz/½ cup double [heavy] cream**

Cream the butter well with the curry powder and add the mango chutney. Grate the cheese. Whip the cream.

Mix together the butter, coconut and grated cheese, and fold in the whipped cream. Serve.

## Pineapple and cream cheese dip

Pineapple and cream cheese together make for a lovely refreshing dip to serve to your guests at a cocktail party.

MAKES 150 G/6 OZ

**150 g/6 oz canned pineapple**
**100 g/4 oz cream cheese**
**2 tablespoons tomato chutney or relish**
**4 tablespoons mayonnaise**

Drain the pineapple and mash with a fork.

Mix the cream cheese with the tomato chutney and mayonnaise, add the mashed pineapple, and serve with small bisbuits [crackers].

## Savouries on sticks

Melon cubes, wrapped in thin strips of Parma Ham.

Chopped celery stalks, stuffed with a mixture of cream cheese and chopped walnuts.

Fresh pineapple cubes with slices of Swiss gruyère cheese.

Small chunks of Spanish chorizo sausage. Cubes of garlic sausage spiked with slices of pickled pimento.

## Les crudités

Les crudités can be found on nearly every restaurant menu in France – from the humblest to the most sophisticated. The dish is a mixture of raw vegetables, prepared with various dressings and sauces, and served as an appetizer or hors d'oeuvre. The choice of vegetables will depend on what is available and on individual taste, but here is a typical selection of vegetables and dressings to serve.

4 SERVINGS

**4 large firm tomatoes**
**½ small cucumber**
**4 tablespoons French dressing**
**chopped parsley**
**4 medium-sized carrots**
**1 shallot**
**6 tablespoons tarragon dressing**
**8 stalks of celery**
**1 head chicory [endive]**
**1 tablespoon lemon juice**
**1 tablespoon olive oil**

Thinly slice the tomatoes and cucumber and arrange them in small separate dishes. Sprinkle with French dressing and chopped parsley. Peel and grate the carrots and shallot and mix them with a little tarragon dressing. Arrange this in another dish. Cut the celery and chicory into fine strips and dress with lemon juice and olive oil. Arrange them in a serving dish. If preferred all the vegetables can be placed together in a large bowl, and the sauces served separately. The vegetables are often served with mayonnaise and rich sauces. They may also be served with sardines, tuna fish, coeur de palmier or artichoke hearts and a slice of ham, pâté or salami.

*Above Crudités make ideal scoops for dips. Use a variety of raw vegetables to make an attractive display for your table.*

# SPREADS

No drinks party is complete without savouries to spread on biscuits [crackers]. Make them attractive as possible with colourful garnishes. Don't prepare them too well in advance or they will become soggy. Try and keep them as fresh as possible.

## Kipper Pâté

This delicious quick and easy-to-prepare pâté makes a tempting tidbit at a party.

6 SERVINGS

**250 g/10 oz packet of frozen kipper fillets**
**1 small onion (chopped very small)**
**100 g/4 oz butter (room temperature)**
**juice of a medium-sized lemon**
**¼ whole nutmeg**
**salt, pepper, paprika**

Cook the kipper fillets according to the instructions on the pack, drain and allow to cool.

Remove the skins and put the fillets

into a mixing bowl. Mash to a pulp with a large fork.

Add onions, lemon juice and butter, and mash again with the fork until all is smooth and creamy.

Add grated nutmeg, and season to taste with salt and pepper.

Chill for one hour.

Spread pâté on small biscuits [crackers], sprinkle with paprika and decorate with slices of stuffed olive or gherkin.

### Cheese and pepper spread

Cheese and pepper spread on biscuits [crackers] makes a tempting snack.

6 SERVINGS

**450 g/1 lb of cheddar cheese (grated)**
**6 spring onions [scallions] (chopped)**
**1 small red pepper (seeded and chopped small)**
**100 g/4 oz of mayonnaise**

Put all the ingredients into a large mixing bowl and blend evenly.

Serve spread on small biscuits [crackers].

### Shrimp pâté

The fresh taste of shrimps makes a delightfully original pâté to serve.

6 SERVINGS

**225 g/½ lb of peeled prawns (thawed if frozen)**
**4 teaspoons of olive oil**
**juice of a small lemon**
**a few gratings of nutmeg**
**salt, and a pinch of cayenne pepper**
**50 g/2 oz of peeled prawns for garnish**
**a little praprika**

Put the prawns, olive oil, lemon juice and nutmeg into the goblet of a liquidizer and blend till you have a smooth paste.

Empty into a bowl and season with salt and cayenne, according to taste. Chill.

Serve spread on savoury biscuits [crackers] and garnish with whole prawns and a sprinkling of paprika.

## CANAPES

These are small, dainty savouries that are served hot or cold as cocktail snacks, appetizers or after a meal. The base of canapés can be small biscuits [crackers], pastry or fried bread, cut into fancy shapes. The toppings should be colourful, tasty and can be meat, fish, eggs or vegetables. Sometimes a thin layer of aspic jelly is spooned over each canapé and this keeps the topping from drying out.

If canapés are served with drinks or before a meal, a selection of different flavours, textures and colours should be made and then arranged on a large tray.

### Crab canapés

A creamy crab mixture on elegant toast fingers, crab canapés make a delicious cocktail savoury.

18 CANAPÉS

**3 tablespoons butter**
**1 tablespoon finely chopped onion**
**1 tablespoon flour**
**150 ml/6 fl oz/¾ cup single [light] cream**
**225 g/½ lb crabmeat, flaked**
**¼ teaspoon salt**
**⅛ teaspoon Tabasco sauce**
**1 teaspoon fresh lemon juice**
**6 slices of toast, crusts removed and each slice cut into 3 fingers**
**1 tablespoon cream cheese**
**½ teaspoon paprika**
**2 teaspoons chopped capers**

In a small saucepan melt 1 tablespoon of butter over moderate heat. When the foam subsides, add the onion and fry for 4 to 5 minutes, or until the onion is light brown in colour.

Remove the saucepan from the heat and stir in the flour. Pour in the cream, return the pan to the heat and bring the cream to the boil, stirring continuously with a wooden spoon. Add the crab, salt, pepper, Tabasco and lemon juice. Bring to the boil again.

Remove the pan from the heat and spread the toast fingers with the crab mixture.

Preheat the grill [broiler] to high. In a small bowl, blend the cream cheese and remaining butter together with a fork to a smooth paste. Add the paprika. Dot a teaspoonful of the cheese paste over the crab mixture.

Place the canapés under the grill [broiler] and cook for 1 minute. Transfer the canapés to a warmed serving dish and garnish with the chopped capers.

### Shrimp canapés

Spicy shrimps on bite-sized squares of fried bread may be served either hot or cold. The quantities of curry powder, cayenne and chilli sauce may be increased if a hotter flavour is desired.

12 CANAPÉS

**50 g/2 oz/¼ cup butter**
**88 g/3½ oz canned shrimps, drained**
**¼ teaspoon curry powder**
**⅛ teaspoon cayenne pepper**
**⅛ teaspoon chilli sauce**
**¼ teaspoon salt**
**juice of ¼ lemon**

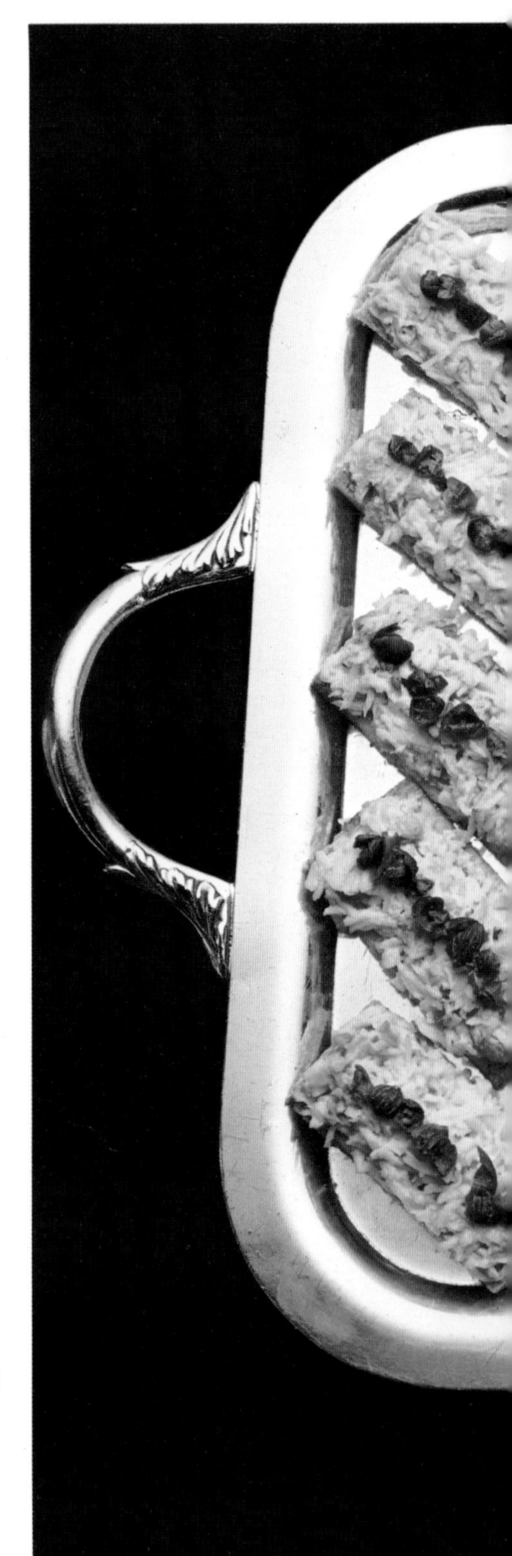

***Right** A tempting selection of canapés for you to make, that will be eagerly eaten by your guests.*

**4 slices fried bread, crusts removed and each slice cut into 3 ovals**
**chopped parsley**

In a small saucepan, melt the butter over moderately low heat. As soon as the foam subsides, add the shrimps, curry powder, cayenne pepper, chilli sauce, salt and lemon juice and simmer gently for 4 minutes

With a slotted spoon, remove the shrimps from the pan and place them on the pieces of fried bread. Garnish each canapé with chopped parsley.

## Lobster canapés

Lobster canapés are made of lobster marinated in oil and vinegar, mixed with a creamy mayonnaise and spread on fingers of toasted bread. They are excellent to serve at a cocktail or drinks party. They look especially attractive if garnished with small crisp lettuce leaves or slices of cucumber.

18 CANAPES

**1 tablespoon wine vinegar**
**3 tablespoons olive oil**
**¼ teaspoon sugar**
**¼ teaspoon salt**

**¼ teaspoon black pepper**
**100 g/4 oz canned lobster, drained and flaked**
**1 tablespoon chopped parsley**
**1 lean bacon slice, grilled until brown and crisp and crumbled**
**1 celery stalk, finely chopped**
**1 teaspoon finely chopped chives**
**⅛ teaspoon cayenne pepper**
**4 to 6 tablespoons mayonnaise**
**6 slices of toast, crusts removed and each slice cut into 3 fingers**

In a small bowl mix the vinegar, oil, sugar, salt and pepper together with a spoon. Place the lobster meat in the bowl, mix well and leave to marinate for at least 1 hour.

With a slotted spoon remove the lobster from the marinade and place it in a small mixing bowl. Discard the marinade. Add the parsley, bacon, celery, chives, cayenne and mayonnaise and mix well together with a fork. Taste for seasoning and add more salt and pepper if necessary.

Spread the mixture on the fingers of toast and serve.

## Spinach and cheese canapés

An unusual and tempting mixture of spinach and cheese on crisp croûtes are delicious served with cocktails. The canapés may be prepared well in advance and reheated by grilling [broiling] just before serving.

24 CANAPES

**1 teaspoon salt**
**675 g/1½ lb spinach, washed and stalks removed**
**4 tablespoons butter**
**½ teaspoon black pepper**
**75 g/3 oz/¾ cup grated cheese**
**1 tablespoon olive oil**
**24 triangles of white bread**
**25 g/1 oz/⅓ cup fine, dry white bread-crumbs**
**2 tablespoons butter, melted**

Half-fill a large saucepan with cold water. Add the salt and bring the water to the boil over high heat. Put the spinach in the pan and reduce the heat to moderate. Cook the spinach for 7 to 12 minutes or until it is tender.

Drain the spinach in a colander and squeeze it dry between two plates. Chop it finely and return it to the saucepan. Add 2 tablespoons of the butter, the pepper and two-thirds of the cheese and stir to mix. Cover the pan and set it aside in a warm place.

In a large frying pan, melt the remaining butter and the oil over moderately high heat. When the foam subsides, add the triangles of bread.

Fry for 10 minutes on each side, or until lightly browned.

Remove the croûtes from the pan with a slotted spoon and place them on kitchen paper towels to drain.

Preheat the grill [broiler] to high.

Place a tablespoon of the spinach and cheese mixture on each croûte and top with the remaining cheese, breadcrumbs and melted butter.

Place the canapés under the grill [broiler] and cook for 2 to 3 minutes or until they are hot and the cheese lightly browned. Serve at once.

## Spicy canapés

Bite-sized squares of toast spread with a spicy cream cheese mixture and quickly baked, spicy canapés are quick and easy to make, and are sure to please your guests.

24 CANAPES

**100 g/4 oz cream cheese**
**1 shallot, minced [ground]**
**1 egg, lightly beaten**
**½ teaspoon Tabasco sauce**
**6 slices of toasted bread, crusts removed and each slice cut into 4 squares**

Preheat the oven to fairly hot Gas Mark 5, 190°C [375°F].

Put the cheese, shallot, egg and Tabasco into a medium-sized mixing bowl. Using a wire whisk or wooden spoon, beat the mixture until it is light and creamy.

Spread the cheese mixture on the squares of toast and place the squares on a baking sheet.

Bake the canapés in the oven for 5 to 10 minutes, or until they are just beginning to brown. Remove the canapés from the oven, transfer them to a warmed serving plate and serve at once.

## Sardine canapés

A tasty combination of sardines, egg and anchovies on squares of white bread and butter, sardine canapés may be prepared well in advance and kept, covered, in the refrigerator until you are ready to serve.

16 CANAPES

**4 slices white bread, crusts removed**
**2 to 4 tablespoons butter**
**1 can sardines, drained of oil**
**¼ teaspoon black pepper**
**½ teaspoon fresh lemon juice**
**2 teaspoons chopped parsley**
**3 hard-boiled eggs, thinly sliced**
**16 anchovy fillets, rolled**

Butter each slice of bread. Cut each slice into 4 squares.

In a small mixing bowl, mash the sardines, pepper, lemon juice and parsley to a paste with a fork.

Spread the mixture on the squares of bread. Place a slice of hard-boiled egg on top of the sardine mixture and garnish with the rolled anchovy fillets.

# VOL-AU-VENTS

This is the basic pastry case which encloses a variety of fillings to make up the classic French vol-au-vent. It is time-consuming to make – but the end result is well worth the effort.

ONE 20 CM [8 IN] VOL-AU-VENT CASE

**450 g/1 lb/4 cups puff pastry, chilled**
**1 egg lightly beaten with ½ teaspoon salt**

Sprinkle a large baking sheet with cold water and set aside. On a lightly floured working surface, roll out the dough to 2.5 cm [1 in] thick.

Using a 20 cm [8 in] oval plate as a guide, with a sharp knife cut out two ovals of dough. Place one oval on the baking sheet. Cut out a smaller oval, for the lid, from the centre of the second piece of dough and set the lid aside.

Using a pastry brush dipped in water, dampen the edges of the large oval of dough on the baking sheet. Place the dough oval, left over from the lid, on top. Gently press the edges together with your finger tips.

Using a knife, flake-up the sides of the dough case (this seals the dough together and helps it to rise).

Place the small oval, which will form the lid, on the baking sheet. Place the baking sheet in the refrigerator and chill the dough for 30 minutes.

Preheat the oven to very hot Gas Mark 9, 240°C [475°F].

Remove the baking sheet from the refrigerator. Using a sharp knife, mark the dough lid into squares.

Brush the top of the dough case and lid with the beaten egg mixture, taking care not to let the egg touch the sides of the dough.

Place the baking sheet in the oven and bake the vol-au-vent for 20 minutes. Remove the baking sheet from the oven and transfer the lid to a wire rack.

Reduce the oven temperature to moderate Gas Mark 4, 180°C [350°F]. Using two spoons, remove and discard

*Cut out two ovals of dough and place one on a baking sheet. Cut out a smaller oval from the second oval.*

*Gently press the edges of the two pieces of dough together, flaking up the sides with a knife to help it rise.*

*When the vol-au-vent is cooked, using spoons, remove the soft dough from the centre of the vol-au-vent case.*

any soft dough from the inside of the vol-au-vent. Return the vol-au-vent to the oven and bake for a further 30 to 40 minutes or until the vol-au-vent is crisp and golden brown.

Remove the vol-au-vent from the oven It is now ready to be filled.

Try the fillings given or make your own variations. You will find them extremely popular with your guests.

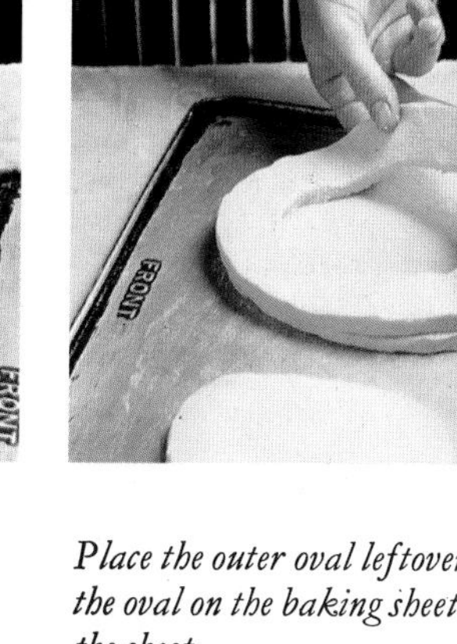

*Place the outer oval leftover from the lid over the oval on the baking sheet. Place the lid on the sheet.*

*With a sharp knife, make a criss-cross pattern across the top of both the vol-au-vent case and the lid.*

*Bake the case again then remove it from the oven. Place the lid next to it. It is now ready to be filled.*

## Vol-au vent filled with aubergines [eggplant]

A vegetarian dish, vol-au-vent with aubergines [eggplants] makes a pleasant change from the more usual vol-au-vent fillings.

4-6 SERVINGS

**3 aubergines [eggplants], peeled, sliced and dègored**
**4 teaspoons salt**
**6 medium-sized onions, thinly sliced and pushed out into rings**
**450 g/1 lb tomatoes, blanched, peeled, seeded and finely chopped**
**75 ml/3 fl oz/$\frac{3}{8}$ cup olive oil**
**6 garlic cloves, crushed**
**1 teaspoon coriander seeds, crushed**
**250 ml/10 fl oz/$1\frac{1}{4}$ cups chicken stock**
**2 tablespoons finely chopped fresh parsley**
**1 tablespoon beurre manié**
**20 cm [8 in] vol-au-vent case, baked**

Put the aubergines [eggplants], salt, onions, tomatoes, oil, garlic, coriander, chicken stock and parsley into a large saucepan. Using a wooden spoon, mix the ingredients together. Set the pan over moderate heat and bring the liquid to the boil. Reduce the heat to low, cover the pan and simmer for 45 minutes or until the aubergines [eggplants] are tender. Remove the pan from the heat.

Pour the mixture through a fine strainer set over a large mixing bowl. Place the vegetables in a medium-sized bowl and set aside.

Preheat the oven to moderate Gas Mark 4, 180°C [350°F].

Return the cooking liquid to the pan and return the pan to the heat. Stirring constantly, add the beurre manié, a little at a time, until the sauce is thick and smooth. Remove the pan from the heat. Add 4 tablespoons of the sauce to the vegetables and, using a wooden spoon, gently stir the mixture. Spoon the mixture into the vol-au-vent case. Set the remaining sauce aside and keep warm. Place the case on a baking sheet and place the baking sheet in the oven. Bake for 5 minutes or until the vol-au-vent is heated through. Remove the baking sheet from the oven. Transfer the vol-au-vent to a warmed serving dish. Pour the remaining sauce into a warmed sauceboat and serve at once, with the vol-au-vent.

## Vol-au-vent filled with scallops

A delightful dish, made with pastry that melts in the mouth, vol-au-vent filled with scallops has a rich, delicate scallop filling. Serve hot, with a lettuce and fennel salad.

4-6 SERVINGS

**25 g/1 oz/2 tablespoons butter**
**12 shallots, finely sliced**
**450 g/1 lb scallops**
**200 ml/8 fl oz/1 cup dry white wine**
**3 lemon slices**
**2 whole cloves**
**1 garlic clove, halved**

**3 tablespoons chopped fresh parsley**
**3 egg yolks**
**¼ teaspoon salt**
**¼ teaspoon black pepper**
**250 ml/10 fl oz/1¼ cups double [heavy] cream**
**25 g/1 oz/2 tablespoons beurre manié**
**200 g/8 oz mushrooms, wiped clean and finely sliced**
**1 tablespoon brandy**
**20 cm [8 in] vol-au-vent case, baked**

Preheat the oven to moderate Gas Mark 4, 180°C [350°F].

In a medium-sized saucepan, melt the butter over moderate heat. When the foam subsides, add the shallots and fry, stirring occasionally, for 3 to 4 minutes or until they are soft and translucent.

Add the scallops, wine, lemon, cloves, garlic and parsley. Increase the heat to high and bring the liquid to the boil. Reduce the heat to low and simmer for 5 minutes. Remove the pan from the heat. Pour the mixture through a fine wire strainer set over a large bowl and discard the lemon, cloves and garlic. Set the contents of the strainer aside.

In a large mixing bowl, mix together the egg yolks, salt, pepper and cream, stirring well to blend. Add the scallop liquid, a little at a time, stirring constantly with a wooden spoon until the ingredients are well blended. Return the mixture to the saucepan and set the pan over moderate heat. Add the beurre manié, a little at a time, stirring constantly until the sauce is thick and smooth.

Stir in the reserved scallop mixture and the mushrooms and cook for 5 minutes, stirring constantly. Remove the pan from the heat.

Warm the brandy and ignite it. When the flames die down, stir the brandy into the mixture. Spoon the mixture into the vol-au-vent case.

Place the case on a baking sheet and place the baking sheet in the oven. Bake for 5 minutes or until the vol-au-vent is heated through. Remove the baking sheet from the oven. Transfer the vol-au-vent to a warmed serving dish and serve.

## Vol-au-vent-filled with chicken and mushrooms

This is a creamy mixture of cooked chicken and mushrooms in a light, crisp pastry case. This is reasonably economical and would make an excellent dish for a drinks party.

4–6 SERVINGS

**25 g/1 oz/2 tablespoons butter**
**2 tablespoons flour**
**200 ml/8 fl oz/1 cup chicken stock**
**50 ml/2 fl oz/¼ cup dry white wine**
**200 g/8 oz button mushrooms, wiped clean and sautéed**
**300 g/12 oz cooked boned chicken, chopped**
**1 canned pimiento, drained and chopped**
**¼ teaspoon salt**
**¼ teaspoon black pepper**
**2 teaspoons lemon juice**
**1 teaspoon dried thyme**
**75 ml/3 fl oz/⅜ cup double [heavy] cream**
**20 cm [8 in] vol-au-vent case, baked**
**1 tablespoon chopped fresh parsley**

Preheat the oven to moderate Gas Mark 4, 180°C [350°].

In a medium-sized saucepan, melt the butter over moderate heat. When the

***Below** Serve this creamy, scallop filled vol-au-vent at your drinks party for a more filling dish.*

***Above*** *Small bouchée cases filled with a creamy lobster, mushroom and sherry mixture make a luxurious appetizer.*

foam subsides, remove the pan from the heat and, with a wooden spoon, stir in the flour to make a smooth paste. Gradually add the stock and wine, stirring constantly and being careful to avoid lumps. Return the pan to the heat and cook, stirring constantly, for 2 to 3 minutes or until the sauce is thick and smooth. Add the mushrooms, chicken, pimiento, salt, pepper, lemon juice and thyme to the pan and cook, stirring occasionally, for 8 to 10 minutes or until all the ingredients are thoroughly combined and the mushrooms and chicken are heated through.

Stir in the cream and remove the pan from the heat. Spoon the mixture into the vol-au-vent case.

Place the case on a baking sheet and place the baking sheet in the oven. Bake for 5 minutes or until the vol-au-vent is heated through. Remove the baking sheet from the oven.

Transfer the vol-au-vent to a warmed serving dish. Sprinkle over the parsley and serve at once.

### Lobster bouchées

Lobster bouchées, with a superb creamy filling, makes a delicious hors d'oeuvre or cocktail bite. The pastry case and béchamel sauce may be prepared in advance and the filling assembled before the bouchées are to be served.

18 SMALL BOUCHEES

**18 small baked hot bouchée cases (small vol-au-vent cases)**
**1 kg/2 lb cooked lobster, shell split, claws cracked and grey sac removed**
**25 g/1 oz/2 tablespoons butter**
**200 g/8 oz mushrooms, wiped clean and sliced**
**2 egg yolks**
**2 tablespoons double [heavy] cream**
**200 ml/10 fl oz/1¼ cups béchamel sauce**
**½ teaspoon salt**
**½ teaspoon black pepper**
**⅛ teaspoon cayenne pepper**
**100 ml/4 fl oz/½ cup sherry**
**2 teaspoons lemon juice**

To make the filling, remove the lobster meat from the shells and claws. Discard the shells and dice the meat. Set aside to use later on.

In a medium-sized frying-pan, melt the butter over moderate heat. When the foam subsides, add the mushrooms and cook, stirring occasionally, for 5 to 6 minutes. With a slotted spoon, remove the mushrooms from the pan and set aside on a plate.

In a small mixing bowl, beat the egg yolks and cream together with a wire whisk. Set aside.

In a medium-sized saucepan, heat the béchamel sauce over moderate heat. Add the diced lobster, mushrooms, salt, pepper and cayenne. Stirring carefully, cook the sauce for 2 to 3 minutes. Do not worry if the sauce is quite thick at this stage.

Remove the pan from the heat. Carefully stir in the egg yolk and cream mixture. Return the pan to low heat and, stirring constantly, cook the sauce gently for 2 minutes. Stir in the sherry and lemon juice and cook for 1 minute. Taste the sauce and add more seasoning if necessary.

Spoon the filling into the hot bouchée cases and serve at once.

# DANISH SANDWICHES

### Salad shrimp

A traditional Danish open sandwich with a mixture of shrimp and mayonnaise is ideal for a more filling snack for a drinks party.

2 SERVINGS

**2 slices rye bread, buttered**
**2 lettuce leaves**
**2 tablespoons mayonnaise**
**100 g/4 oz cooked and peeled shrimps**
**2 twists of lemon**
**2 sprigs of parsley**
**a little paprika**

Place a lettuce leaf flat on each piece of bread. Place a line of shrimps diagonally across the centre of each slice. Pipe mayonnaise either side of the shrimps and then fill the corners with additional shrimps. Place a twist of lemon in the centre and sprigs of watercress either side. Sprinkle with a little paprika.

### The mariner

Rollmop herrings are delicious on rye bread. If necessary use cocktail sticks to secure them.

2 SERVINGS

**2 slices buttered rye bread**
**6 strips rollmop herring**
**6 slices of tomato**
**6 onion rings**
**2 sprigs parsley**

Arrange 3 herring fillets side by side, diagonally on each piece of bread, and tuck a tomato slice in between each herring. Place the onion rings over the top and garnish with a sprig of parsley.

### The tivoli

Generously top buttered rye bread with eggs, tomatoes, cod's roe and mayonnaise for an imaginative open sandwich.

2 SERVINGS

**2 slices buttered rye bread**
**2 lettuce leaves**
**6 slices of hard-boiled egg**
**8 slices of tomato**
**25 g/1 oz smoked cod's roe**
**1 tablespoon mayonnaise**

Place a lettuce leaf on each piece of bread. Arrange the egg slices along one edge and the slices of tomato along the other. Pipe the cod's roe in a row of dots down the centre, and top with piped mayonnaise.

### Danish delight

This mouthwatering concoction will be quickly eaten. Be sure to make plenty.

2 SERVINGS

**2 slices buttered rye bread**
**4 small slices cold cooked pork**
**2 small lettuce leaves**
**1 tablespoon pickled red cabbage**
**2 slices of orange (with peel)**
**2 prunes**

Place 2 slices of pork overlapping on each piece of bread. Place a piece of lettuce in one corner and fill it with red cabbage Place an orange twist in the other corner with a prune.

### Hans Anderson

Remember to make your open sandwiches as attractive as possible. You should be by now inspired to start inventing some toppings of your own.

2 SERVINGS

**2 slices buttered rye bread**
**2 slices liver pâté**
**2 small pieces lettuce leaf**
**4 raw button mushrooms,**
**4 raw button mushrooms, sliced**
**2 slices of tomato**
**2 gherkins**
**2 bacon slices, crisply fried and drained**

Place the slices of pâté on the buttered bread, then in one corner of each piece of bread lay the sliced mushrooms. In the opposite corner lay a tomato slice and a gherkin cut into a fan shape. Arrange the bacon slices diagonally, across the top.

### The Copenhagen

The combination of creamed horseradish, orange and prunes makes an original topping.

2 SERVINGS

**2 slices buttered rye bread**
**6 slices pork luncheon meat**
**1 tablespoon creamed horseradish**
**2 slices of orange (with peel)**
**4 prunes, soaked and stoned**
**2 sprigs watercress**

Fold the slices of luncheon meat into rolls and place 3 side on each piece of bread. Spoon the creamed horseradish into the centre of each roll and place a twisted orange slice on top. Arrange a prune on either side. and add a sprig of watercress to one side.

***Below*** *Celery with red caviar, cream cheese, chives and parsley is an elegant yet economical appetizer.*

### Celery fritters

Celery pieces, parboiled, dipped in butter and fried, make an excellent crisp vegetable and they are particularly good served with a piquant sauce.

4 SERVINGS

**1 or 2 heads of celery**
**1 or 2 heads of celery batter**
**125 g/5 oz/1¼ cups flour**
**1 teaspoon salt**
**2 tablespoons brown ale**
**100 ml/4 fl oz/½ cup water**
**oil for deep frying**

Prepare and parboil the celery for 10 minutes.

Sift the flour and salt into a small mixing bowl. Make a well in the centre and pour in the ale and water. Using a wooden spoon or a wire whisk, mix in the liquid. Beat well until the mixture is smooth and creamy. Cover the batter and leave it at room temperature for 30 minutes.

Heat the oil in a deep-frying pan. Drain the celery and cut it into small pieces. Dip the celery pieces in the batter. Drop into the hot oil and fry until golden. Drain the fritters on a plate lined with kitchen paper towels. Serve hot.

### Celery with red caviar

An elegant and simple appetizer, celery with red caviar takes only minutes to prepare and can be made an hour or so before serving. It can be accompanied, in a separate dish, by black olives.

4-6 SERVINGS

**2 small heads of celery (or about 10 stalks)**
**200 g/8 oz full-fat cream cheese**
**2 tablespoons chopped chives**
**2 tablespoons chopped fresh parsley**
**88 g/3½ oz jar red caviar**
**½ teaspoon white pepper**

Clean the celery and, on a chopping board, cut each stalk in three, crosswise. Set aside in a serving dish.

In a medium-sized mixing bowl, combine the cream cheese, chives, parsley, red caviar and pepper, beating to blend well.

Spread a little of the cream cheese mixture on to each celery piece and refrigerate for 30 minutes before serving.

***Right*** *Danish open sandwiches make tasty snacks for a party.*

# BUFFET PARTY

### New England clam chowder

New England clam chowder is a delicious, rich dish. Serve with warm crusty bread and butter.

8 SERVINGS

**Three 200 g/8 oz canned minced clams**
**450 g/1 lb canned baby clams**
**2 medium-sized onions**
**50 g/2 oz/4 tablespoons butter**
**500 ml/1 pt/2½ cups water**
**4 large potatoes**
**½ teaspoon Worcestershire sauce**
**250 ml/10 fl oz/1¼ cups milk**
**salt and pepper**
**250 ml/10 fl oz/1¼ cups double [heavy] cream**

Strain the juice from the cans of clams and reserve. Slice the onions and sauté in butter until soft and transparent. Set aside.

Peel the potatoes. Thinly slice two of the potatoes and cook in the clam juice until tender, then mash them in to the clam juice. Parboil the other potatoes, cut into small cubes, and add to the clam juice mixture.

Put in the Worcestershire sauce. Add the milk and onions and gently simmer for 5-7 minutes. Now add the clams, and salt and pepper to taste. Cook for 2 minutes over a low heat. Remove the pan from the stove and gradually stir in the cream. Return the pan to a low heat and cook until the cream is warmed. Do not let the mixture come to the boil.

Serve immediately.

# HERRINGS

Herrings are amongst the most popular items on the Scandinavian smorgasbord. They also make excellent nibbles for buffet parties. Most good delicatessen shops stock either salted herrings, or herrings in brine. These should always be soaked in water for 6-8 hours before using. The matjes herring is probably the best known abroad. It is sometimes sold by weight but more often in cans. Unlike the other varieties this herring need not be soaked before use, and could be substituted for salted herrings.

### Marinated smoked buckling

12 SERVINGS

**12 smoked buckling or kippers**
FOR MARINADE
**6 tablespoons tomato purée [paste]**
**6 tablespoons vinegar**
**6 tablespoons olive oil**
**6 tablespoons water**
**3 bayleaves**
**1½ teaspoons salt**
**freshly ground black pepper**
**3 teaspoons sugar**
TO GARNISH
**6 tablespoons chopped chives**

Remove the head, skin and bones from the bucklings or kippers and arrange them in strips on a serving dish. In a screw-top jar put together the ingredients for the marinade and shake well. Pour over the smoked buckling fillets, and leave covered in a cool place for 1-2 hours.

Sprinkle with the chopped chives before serving.

### Piquant herring

12 SERVINGS

**6 large matjes herrings**
**6 hard-boiled eggs**
**6 large, red tomatoes**
FOR SAUCE
**3 tablespoons made English mustard**
**3 tablespoons sugar**
**6 tablespoons wine vinegar**
**150 ml/6 fl oz/¾ cup olive oil**
**3 large sweet pickled gherkin**
TO GARNISH
**chopped fresh dill or parsley**

Cut the matjes herrings in half and roll each half up. Place these in the middle of a serving dish. Cut the eggs and tomatoes into wedges and place around the herrings. Mix together the mustard, sugar and vinegar, and beat well. Add the oil, little by little, as for mayonnaise. Finely chop the gherkins and add it to the sauce. Pour over the herrings and garnish with the dill or parsley.

Serve very cold.

### Soused herrings

12 SERVINGS

**12 fresh herrings**
**150 ml/6 fl oz/¾ cup milk**
**12 tablespoons oatmeal**
**100 g/4 oz/8 tablespoons butter**
**salt and freshly ground pepper**
FOR MARINADE
**500 ml/1 pt/2½ cups wine vinegar**
**250 ml/10 fl oz/1¼ cups water**
**300 g /12 oz/1½ cups sugar**
**6 bayleaves**
**4 cloves**
TO GARNISH
**sprigs of fresh dill**
**1 small onion, finely chopped**

Clean the herrings, remove the heads and trim the fins and tails. Wash them and drain well. Dip in the milk and coat with oatmeal. Season with salt and pepper.

Heat the butter in a large frying-pan and fry the herrings until they are golden brown on both sides. Remove them from the frying-pan and set aside to cool.

Put all the ingredients for the marinade into a saucepan and heat until the sugar has dissolved. Remove from the heat and cool.

Pour the cold marinade over the fish and garnish with the dill sprigs and the chopped onion.

### Herrings in sherry

12 SERVINGS

**6 matjes herrings**
**6 tablespoons sugar**
**8 tablespoons water**
**150 ml/6 fl oz/¾ cup sherry**
**4 tablespoons wine vinegar**
**2 medium-sized onions**
**8 crushed white peppercorns**
**fresh sprigs of dill**

Cut the herrings crosswise into 2.5 cm [1 in] wide strips and place them on a serving dish.

Dissolve the sugar in the water before adding the sherry and the vinegar. Leave to cool. Slice the onions, separate into rings and place over the fish with the crushed peppercorns.

Pour the cold marinade over and refrigerate for 2-3 hours before serving. Garnish with the sprigs of dill.

### Fillet of beef in a pastry case

Fillet of beef in a pastry case will provide an excellent centrepiece for a buffet party.

12 SERVINGS

**2¼ kg/4½ lbs fillet of beef**
**freshly ground pepper**
**75 g/3 oz button mushrooms**
**4 tablespoons chopped parsley**
**½ teaspoon salt**
**150 g/6 oz good quality liver pâté**
**300 g/12 oz puff pastry**
**1 egg**

Heat oven to Gas Mark 6, 200°C [400°F].

Trim off all the excess fat and sinew from the meat. Roll into a neat bolster and tie with fine string at intervals to secure the shape. Dust with pepper. Heat the butter in a frying-pan and brown the meat all over.

Transfer the beef to a roasting tin and roast in the oven for 10 minutes. Take out and leave to cool. Remove the string. Wipe clean and slice the mushrooms, and sauté in the butter left from the meat, mix with the parsley and a little salt and leave to cool. Roll out the pastry to a rectangle about 3 mm [⅛ in] thick, and large enough to easily cover the meat. Spread the pâté and the mushrooms over the top and sides of the fillet, and place it, pâté side down, in the centre of the pastry. Then spread pâté on the remaining side. Beat the egg and brush along the edges of the pastry, and fold the pastry over the meat, pressing the two sides firmly together. Brush the pastry ends with egg and fold up, cutting away any surplus pastry. Use this for making decorative leaves.

Place the fillet of beef on a baking tray, join down, brush with egg, and place the pastry leaves in the centre of the pastry. Place in the oven for 30-40 minutes until the pastry is golden brown.

Serve hot or cold.

## Tandoori chicken pieces

Tandoori chicken is one of the most popular chicken dishes of India. It is ideal for a more substantial dish for a buffet party.

12 SERVINGS

**Three 1.2 kg/2½ lb chickens**
**salt and pepper**
**250 ml/10 fl oz/1¼ cups plain yoghurt**
**1 teaspoon hot chilli powder**
**3 cloves of garlic, crushed**
**¼ teaspoon ground ginger**
**¼ teaspoon ground coriander**
**1 teaspoon mild curry powder**
**juice of 1 lemon**
**75 g/3 oz/6 tablespoons butter**
**6 tablespoons sugar**

Heat oven to Gas Mark 5,190°C [375°F].

Joint the chickens and wipe them dry. Season with salt and pepper. Make the marinade by mixing the yoghurt, chilli powder, garlic ,cloves, ginger, coriander, curry powder and the lemon juice.

Mix well and marinate the chicken joints in this for 4 hours, turning several times. Melt the butter and the sugar in a frying pan and fry the chicken pieces until they are brown on all sides.

Wrap each chicken piece in foil and cook in the oven for 20 minutes. Heat the marinade and serve with the chicken, baked potatoes and beetroot [beet] salad.

## Chicken salad with melon and mango dressing

Chicken served with fresh melon and mango chutney makes an interesting salad.

12 SERVINGS

**Two 1¾ kg/3½ lb chickens**
**1 onion sliced**
**2 carrots, scraped and sliced**
**1 bouquet garni**
**½ teaspoon salt**
FOR DRESSING
**500 ml/1 pt/2½ cups mayonnaise**
**250 ml/10 fl oz/1¼ cups double [heavy] cream**
**8 tablespoons mango chutney**
TO GARNISH
**1 Honeydew or 2 Charantais melons**
**2 red peppers**

***Below*** *Chicken salad with mango and melon makes an unusual dish.*

In a large saucepan cover the chickens with water, add the onion, carrots, bouquet garni and the salt. Bring to the boil, reduce the heat and simmer for 40 minutes. Take off the heat and leave the chickens to cool in the liquid. When they are cold, take them out of the saucepan, remove the skin and pull the meat off the bones. Place the meat in a neat row on a large serving dish.

Cut the melon into narrow boat-shaped pieces and remove the pips and the rind. Arrange on the serving dish with the chicken.

Whip the cream and mix with the mayonnaise. Add the mango chutney and season with salt and pepper.

Wash the peppers, remove the cores and the seeds. Slice into rings and arrange them over the chicken and melon on the dish.

Serve with a rice and nut salad, a tomato salad and a plain green salad.

## Fried whitebait

This is a basic recipe for preparing these tasty little fish. Served with a selection of salads, fried whitebait makes an excellent buffet dish.

4-6 SERVINGS

**450 g/1 lb whitebait or small fresh sardines**
**63 g/2½ oz/½ cup plus 2 tablespoons flour**
**1 teaspoon salt**
**½ teaspoon freshly milled black pepper**
**vegetable oil for deep frying**
TO GARNISH
**parsley sprigs**
**lemon slices**

Rinse the whitebait in cold water then drain well and dry on absorbent kitchen paper.

Put the whitebait, flour and seasoning into a large bag and shake until each fish is evenly coated with seasoned flour.

Transfer the fish to a frying basket, shaking well to remove all the surplus flour. Heat the oil for deep frying. Fry the whitebait a few at a time in deep fat, taking care to shake the frying basket frequently to prevent the fish from sticking together.

Drain each batch well on absorbent kitchen paper. Serve garnished with parsley and lemon slices.

## Melons with mulled wine

A simple dessert, melons with mulled wine is cool and refreshing. It makes an ideal dish for a buffet party.

4 SERVINGS

**2 small melons**
**250 ml/10 fl oz/1¼ cups sweet red wine**
**slice of orange**
**slice of lemon**
**1 small stick cinnamon**
**pinch of allspice**
**2 cloves**
**2 teaspoons honey**

Wrap the whole melons in aluminium foil and chill. Heat the wine with the fruit, spices and honey and simmer for 10-15 minutes. Strain and chill well. Cut the melons in half and scoop out the seeds. Place each half in a shallow fruit dish. If the melon is too large to fit a dish, cut a very thin slice from each base so that the melon will stand firmly on a plate. Spoon the chilled wine mixture into the melons just before serving.

## Peppermint-ice grapefruit

A delightfully fresh-tasting dish, peppermint-ice grapefruit makes an interesting hors d'oeuvre.

4 SERVINGS

**1 egg white**
**50 g/2 oz/¼ cup castor [fine] sugar**
**4 grapefruit**
**4-8 teaspoons Crème de Menthe**

Place the egg white in a small plate or saucer. Dip the rims of 4 serving glasses in the egg white and then in the castor [fine] sugar. Stand the glasses upright and set aside for about 1 hour until the egg white and sugar harden and form an attractive rim.

Meanwhile, using a sharp knife, remove and discard the zest and white pith from each grapefruit. Cut out each segment of grapefruit, leaving behind the pith. This is best done over a bowl to catch the juice.

Carefully fill the prepared glasses with the grapefruit segments and juice. Add 1-2 teaspoons of Crème de Menthe to each glass. Chill for 1-2 hours before serving.

## Pineapple pol

Pineapple pol makes a delectable dessert for a buffet party.

SERVES 4

**2 small ripe pineapples**
**½ small cucumber**
**¼ small honeydew melon**
**Roquefort dressing**

Cut each pineapple in half lengthwise, through the green spikes. Cut out the pineapple flesh and chop it coarsely. Dice the cucumber and the melon flesh or, if you have a melon or Parisienne cutter, scoop the melon out in little balls. Pile the prepared fruit into each pineapple half and chill well. Dress with a little Roquefort dressing just before serving or with plain French dressing.

## Baked avocado with crab

Baked avocados filled with crabmeat make a delicious combination. Serve hot.

SERVES 4

**1 shallot**
**300 g/12 oz frozen or canned white crabmeat with cartilage removed**
**250 ml/10 fl oz/1¼ cups béchamel sauce**
**1 tablespoon tomato purée [paste]**
**2 tablespoons lemon juice**
**25 g/1 oz/2 tablespoons butter**
**2 avocados**
TO GARNISH
**1 teaspoon chopped parsley**
**½ teaspoon paprika**

Heat the oven to Gas Mark 5, 190°C [375°F].

Peel and finely chop the shallot and mix it in a small saucepan with the crabmeat, béchamel sauce, tomato purée [paste] and lemon juice. Warm through slowly over low heat. Halve the avocados and remove the stones. Pile the crabmeat mixture into the cavity of each avocado half and place them in an ovenproof dish. Pour a little water around the avocados and cover with a lid or with aluminium foil. Place on the top shelf of the preheated oven and bake for 15 minutes. Sprinkle with parsley and paprika just before serving.

## Grilled mussels with breadcrumbs

An unusual dish, grilled mussels with breadcrumbs makes a delightful appetizer for a buffet party.

SERVES 4

**1 quart/2½ pints mussels**
**1 shallot**
**200 ml/8 fl oz/1 cup dry white wine**
**½ teaspoon salt**
**¼ teaspoon pepper**
**3-4 sprigs parsley**
**1 bay leaf**
**38 g/1½ oz/3 tablespoons butter**
**75 g/3 oz/1½ cups fine fresh breadcrumbs**

Heat the grill [broiler] at its highest setting. Scrub the mussels very thoroughly under cold running water and remove the beards. Discard any mussels which are not tightly closed, as they are not fit to eat. Peel and chop the shallot. Put the mussels in a large saucepan and add the shallot, wine, salt, pepper, parsley and bay leaf. Cover tightly. Heat over a high flame for 8-10 minutes or until the mussels have opened. Any mussels which do not open must be discarded. Take the mussels out of the saucepan and remove one shell from each. Place the mussels on their remaining shells in a shallow ovenproof dish. Sprinkle with the breadcrumbs and put a dot of butter on each mussel. Grill [broil] for 3-4 minutes until the breadcrumbs are crisp and golden brown. Serve immediately.

***Left*** *Grilled mussels, fried whitebait and peppermint-ice grapefruit are tasty snacks to serve at a buffet party.*

## Devilled scallops

A pungent, spicy way to serve scallops that will delight your guests.

4 SERVINGS

**8 scallops**
**1 shallot**
**1 clove of garlic**
**250 ml/10 fl oz/1¼ cups milk**
**25 g/1 oz/2 tablespoons butter**
**2 tablespoons flour**
**½ level teaspoon curry powder**
**1 tablespoon sherry**
**dash Tabasco sauce**
**4 tablespoons fine fresh breadcrumbs**

Heat the grill [broiler] at its highest setting. Remove the scallops from their shells and rinse well. Keep 4 shells for serving. Peel and finely chop the shallot and garlic. Dice the scallops and place them in a saucepan with the milk, shallot and garlic. Bring to the boil slowly over moderate heat then lower the flame and simmer for about 10 minutes. Strain off the liquid and reserve. Meanwhile melt the butter in a small saucepan. Stir in the flour and curry powder; then add the reserved liquid, a little at a time. Bring to the boil, stirring continuously, until the mixture thickens. Add the diced scallops, the sherry and Tabasco sauce, and mix well. Fill the 4 shells with the mixture and sprinkle with breadcrumbs. Grill [broil] for 2-3 minutes until the breadcrumbs are golden brown. Serve immediately.

## Roquefort pear salad

Cheese and fruit make a delectable combination. See how popular this Roquefort pear salad is.

4 SERVINGS

**4 ripe dessert pears**
**lemon juice**
**50 g/2 oz/4 tablespoons Roquefort or other blue cheese**
**50 g/2 oz/4 tablespoons cream cheese**
**2 tablespoons mayonnaise**
**1 tablespoon chopped walnuts**
**a little single [light] cream or milk**
**salt and pepper**
TO GARNISH
**lettuce leaves**
**paprika**

Peel and halve the pears, scoop out the cores with a spoon, and dip the fruit quickly in lemon juice to preserve its colour. Place on a serving dish. Mash the Roquefort or blue cheese with the cream cheese and mayonnaise. Add the walnuts, then soften the dressing with sufficient milk or cream to give a coating consistency. Season to taste, and spoon the dressing over the pears.

Make a loose tent-covering of foil over the dish and refrigerate for up to 6 hours. Do not deep-freeze.

Garnish with a few crisp lettuce leaves and paprika.

## Mushroom cocktail

Mushrooms in a mayonnaise sauce makes a super addition to your buffet table.

4 SERVINGS

**225 g/½ lb button mushrooms**
**125 ml/5 fl oz water**
**salt**
**1 teaspoon butter**
**4 tablespoons mayonnaise**
**3 tablespoons double [heavy] cream**
**2 teaspoons horseradish sauce**
**few drops of Worcestershire sauce**
**1 teaspoon lemon juice**
**black pepper**
**heart of 1 small lettuce**
TO GARNISH
**cucumber slices**

Wash the mushrooms, and halve or quarter any large ones. Put them into a saucepan with the water, a pinch of salt and the butter. Cover, bring to the boil, and simmer for about 10 minutes. Remove the mushrooms from the liquid and chill them. Cook the mushroom liquid in an open pan until it is reduced to about 1 tablespoon. Blend together the mayonnaise, cream, cooled mushroom liquid, horseradish sauce, Worcestershire sauce and lemon juice. Season to taste with salt and pepper.

Refrigerate the mushrooms and dressing separately for up to 2 days. The dressing cannot be deep frozen because it contains mayonnaise.

Shred the lettuce finely and put in the base of four glasses. Blend the mushrooms and dressing together, spoon into the glasses, garnish with cucumber slices.

***From left to right: top row** Mushroom cocktail, Florida cocktail, French bean and egg salad, chilled melon and pineapple.*
***Centre** Jamaican grapefruit.*
***Bottom row** Globe artichokes with curry mayonnaise and Roquefort pear salad.*

## Florida cocktail

This refreshing dessert is just right for a buffet party. A time honoured favourite of many.

4 SERVINGS

**1 large grapefruit**
**3 large oranges**
**1 lime**
**sugar optional**
TO DECORATE
**1 small lime, sliced**

Peel the grapefruit and oranges and remove the segments, catching the juice in a bowl. Squeeze the juice from the lime and add to the juice in the bowl together with the fruit segments. Mix well, add sugar if necessary, and arrange in four individual small glasses.

Refrigerate for up to 8 hours. Do not deep freeze.

Decorate each glass with a slice of lime before serving, if these are used.

## Savoury stuffed courgettes [zucchini]

4 SERVINGS

Courgettes [zucchini] stuffed with a tomato and mushroom mixture make an appetizing dish.

**4 medium-to-large courgettes [zucchini]**
**salt**
**1 tablespoon oil**
**1 small onion, finely chopped**
**1 slice bacon, derinded and chopped**
**100 g/¼ lb mushrooms, chopped**
**3 tomatoes, chopped and peeled**
**1 tablespoon chopped parsley**
**1 clove of garlic, crushed**
**pepper**

Cook the whole unpeeled courgettes [zucchini] in boiling salted water for 10 minutes. Drain. When the are cool enough to handle, cut them in half, scoop out the seeds, and chop the flesh roughly. Heat the oil in a pan, and fry the onion and bacon for about 5 minutes until golden. Add the mushrooms and cook for a further 5 minutes. Stir in the tomatoes, chopped courgettes [zucchini], parsley garlic and seasoning, cover and simmer gently for 20 minutes. Spoon the tomato mixture back into the courgette [zucchini] cases and place in a greased ovenproof dish.

The covered dish may be stored at room temperature for up to 6 hours, refrigerated for up to 1-2 days, or deep-frozen.

Heat oven to Gas Mark 5, 190°C [375°F].

Bake, uncovered for 30 minutes. Serve to your guests piping hot.

## Globe artichokes with curry mayonnaise

An elegant vegetable dish for your buffet party, globe artichokes with curry mayonnaise is as appetizing as it is unusual.

4 SERVINGS

**4 globe artichokes**
**salt**
**250 ml/½ pt/1¼ cups mayonnaise**
**2 teaspoons mild curry powder**
**squeeze of lemon juice**
**1 tablespoon mango chutney, finely chopped**

Wash the artichokes well in cold water and trim off any stalks to the base. Cook the artichokes in boiling salted water for 45 minutes or until a leaf can be pulled out easily. Drain and allow to cool. Blend the mayonnaise with the curry powder, lemon juice and chutney.

The artichokes can be left at room temperature for up to 12 hours, or refrigerated for up to 2 days. The mayonnaise sauce will keep in a covered container in the refrigerator for a week. Do not deep-freeze either the sauce or the artichokes.

Serve the artichokes on individual plates and hand the sauce around seperately.

## Jamaican grapefruit

The rich, exotic taste of brown sugar and rum and grapefruit makes a colourful dish for your buffet table.

4 SERVINGS

**2 large grapefruit**
**3 tablespoons brown sugar**
**3 tablespoons dark rum**
TO DECORATE
**4 glacé cherries**

Cut the grapefruit in half. Remove all the segments and put into a bowl. Sprinkle with the brown sugar and rum, and mix well. Pile the mixture back into the grapefruit skins.

Refrigerate the mixture for up to 6 hours, but do not deep-freeze.

Decorate each grapefruit half with a glacé cherry just before serving.

## Chilled melon and pineapple

Refreshing and cool, chilled melon and pineapple are everybody's firm favourite.

SERVES 6 SERVINGS

**1 small pineapple or**
**450 g/1 lb canned pineapple pieces or cubes**
**1 small medium-sized melon**
**1 tablespoon lemon juice**
**sugar**
TO DECORATE
**mint sprigs optional**

Cut the fresh pineapple into slices. Peel, remove the core, cut the flesh into pieces and put into a bowl. If you are using the canned pineapple drain well. Cut a slice off the top of the melon and remove the seeds. Scoop out the flesh, using either a Parisienne cutter to make balls, or a spoon. Put the melon flesh into the bowl with the pineapple, together with any melon juice. Mix well and add the mint, lemon juice and sugar to taste. Pile the pineapple and melon back into the melon skin.

Cover the melon and keep at room temperature for up to 6 hours, but chill for 1½ hours before serving. Do not deep-freeze.

Decorate the melon with the sprigs of mint before serving, if these are used.

# PATES

## Hare and rabbit terrine

This rich, coarse pâté is so delicious served with hot toast and a tossed green salad.

12 SERVINGS

**1 small hare or 1 large rabbit about 1½ kg/3 lb, skinned**
**225 g/½ lb lean pork**
**338 g/¾ lb fatty bacon, de-rinded**
**1 large onion**
**1 tablespoon chopped parsley**
**1 teaspoon chopped fresh thyme or ¼ teaspoon dried**
**1-2 cloves of garlic, crushed**
**salt and freshly milled black pepper**
**4 tablespoons red wine**
**2 tablespoons brandy optional**
**4 slices streaky bacon, derinded**

Heat oven to Gas Mark 3, 170°C [325°F].

Bone the hare or rabbit and cut the back meat carefully into strips. Put this on one side and mince [grind] the pork, bacon and onion. Add the parsley, thyme, garlic seasoning, wine and brandy, and mix together until well-blended. Place

***Right*** *Chicken liver and bacon pâté, and aubergine pâté are delicious as well as being unusual. Pâtés are always everybody's favourites at parties.*

half the mixture in the bottom of a large well-greased terrine or earthenware casserole. Lay the reserved strips of meat from the back of the hare and the bacon slices on top, and cover with the remaining minced mixture. Cover the dish with foil and then a lid. Stand the dish in a roasting tin containing 2.5 cm [1 in] of cold water.

Bake for 2½ hours. Remove from the oven, take off the lid and place weight on top of the foil.

Refrigerate for at least 6 hours before serving. It can be kept refrigerated for up to 5 days, or deep-frozen.

Serve sliced, with hot toast or French bread and butter.

Note: the bones from the hare, on which quite a bit of meat will remain, can be used to make a delicious soup.

## Chicken liver and bacon pâté

Chicken liver and bacon combine to make a mouth watering pâté. You can prepare this dish well in advance for it will keep for up to 4 days in a refrigerator.

4-6 SERVINGS

**100 g/¼ lb chicken liver**
**100 g/¼ lb fatty bacon, derinded**
**1 small onion, chopped**

**1 clove of garlic, crushed**
**63 g/2½ oz/5 tablespoons butter**
**125 ml/5 fl oz milk**
**1 blade mace or a good pinch of ground mace**
**1 bay leaf**
**2-3 peppercorns**
**13 g/½ oz/2 tablespoons flour**
**½ teaspoon anchovy essence**
**1 teaspoon prepared mustard**
**salt and pepper**
TO SEAL
**50 g/2 oz butter melted**

Heat oven to Gas Mark 4, 180°C [350°F].

Gently fry the liver, bacon, onion and garlic in 50 g/2 oz/4 tablespoons of the butter for about 10 minutes. Remove from the heat, and either purée in a blender or mince [grind]. Put the milk into a saucepan with the mace, bay leaf and peppercorns.

Bring slowly to the boil, remove the heat, and leave for 5 minutes. Melt the remaining butter in a saucepan, add the flour and cook for 1 minute. Gradually add the strained milk and bring to the boil, stirring all the time until it thickens. Remove from the heat and stir in the meat mixture, anchovy essence and mustard. Season to taste. Turn into a small, well-greased terrine and cover with a lid or foil. Stand in a roasting tin containing 2.5 cm [1 in] of cold water and bake in a moderate oven for 1 hour. Allow to cool, then spoon the melted butter over it.

Refrigerate for up to 3-4 days or deep-freeze.

Serve from the terrine with hot toast and butter.

## Aubergine [eggplant] pâté

Amaze your guests with this original aubergine [eggplant] pâté. Such a welcome change from the normal flavoured pâtés.

4-6 SERVINGS

**2 large aubergines [eggplants]**
**4 tablespoons olive oil**
**juice of 1 lemon**
**1 clove of garlic, crushed**
**salt and pepper**
TO GARNISH
**onion rings**

Heat oven to Gas Mark 4, 180°C [350°F].

Lightly score the aubergine [eggplant] skins. Put the aubergines [eggplants] on a baking tray, and bake for 1¼ hours or until they are completely soft. When they are cool enough to handle, cut in half and scoop out the pulp. Put this into a bowl and pound or mash until it is fairly smooth. Beat in the oil gradually, then add the lemon juice, crushed garlic, and seasoning to taste.

Cover and refrigerate for up to 3-4 days, or deep-freeze.

Garnish with onion rings, and serve with hot toast or French bread and butter.

## Smoked salmon mousse

This is a lovely way to make use of those end bits of smoked salmon sold quite cheaply at many delicatessen counters. For a really festive touch you could garnish the mousse most attractively with bands of tiny petit pois and red caviar.

**100 g/4 oz smoked salmon pieces**
**4 tablespoons single [light] cream**
**1 teaspoon lemon juice**
**salt**
**freshly ground black pepper**
**freshly grated nutmeg**
**3 tablespoons liquid aspic**
**1 egg white**
**125 ml/5 fl oz/⅝ cup double [heavy] cream**

Chop the smoked salmon coarsely. Put it into a blender, or through a food mill, together with the single [light] cream, lemon juice, a little salt, freshly ground black pepper and nutmeg. Blend it to a smooth purée then beat in 3 tablespoons of liquid aspic.

Whisk the double [heavy] cream until it is soft but firm, then fold it into the salmon mixture. Whisk the egg white until stiff but not dry and add it to the mixture. Taste and season again if necessary.

Pour the mousse into a small deep serving dish or individual ramekins and chill until set.

Serve with brown bread and butter or slices of toast.

## Avocado mousse

This mousse looks as good as it tastes when turned out of its mould and served on a bed of lettuce leaves. Decorate it with paper-thin slices of cucumber, tomato wedges and black olives.

**Half a chicken stock cube**
**1 ripe avocado pear**
**juice of 1 lemon**
**½ teaspoon finely chopped chives**
**½ teaspoon dried tarragon**
**½ teaspoon onion juice**
**a dash of Tabasco**
**6 g/¼ oz powdered gelatine**
**2 tablespoons water**
**125 ml/5 fl oz/⅝ cup double [heavy] cream**
**salt**
**freshly ground black pepper**

Dissolve the stock cube in 125ml/5 fl oz/⅝ cup of boiling water. Peel, stone and dice the avocado roughly. Put the diced avocado into an electric blender together with the stock, lemon juice, herbs, onion juice and Tabasco, and blend until smooth, or pass the mixture through a nylon sieve. Pour into a bowl.

Sprinkle the gelatine over 2 tablespoons of water in a cup and leave for 5 minutes. When softened, place the cup in a bowl of hot water and stir until the gelatine is completely dissolved and the liquid is quite clear. When it is cool beat the dissolved gelatine into the avocado mixture. Whip the cream lightly then fold it into the avocado mixture. Add salt and pepper to taste – the mixture should be highly seasoned.

When the mousse is cold but not set, pour into individual ramekins or one larger mould. Chill until set in the refrigerator.

To turn out the mould, dip into very hot water for a few seconds and invert on to a plate. Serve very cold.

## Tuna stuffed lemons

Tangy lemons filled with a fresh-tasting fish mixture make a delicious hors d'oeuvre.

2 SERVINGS

**2 large lemons**
**175 g/7 oz canned tuna fish, drained**
**50 g/2 oz/4 tablespoons butter**
**a pinch of dried thyme**
**1 teaspoon Dijon mustard**
**½ teaspoon paprika**
**salt and freshly ground black pepper**
**1 egg white**
**chopped parsley**

First slice the tops off the lemons and set them aside. Slice a little off the other end so the lemons will stand upright. Scoop out all the pulp and place in a sieve resting over a bowl. Press the juice through.

In another bowl mash the drained tuna with the butter, then add the mustard and seasonings. Stir in the lemon juice and finally whip the egg white until stiff and fold it into the mixture.

Taste to check the seasonings, fill the lemons with the mixture and decorate each with chopped parsley. Chill for 30 minutes before serving.

*Above Tuna stuffed lemons are really different and delicious. The tangy taste of the lemons and the fresh taste of the tuna fish combine to make a perfect hors d'oeuvre for a buffet party.*

## Courgettes [zucchini] à la Grecque

Always choose small, even-sized courgettes [zucchini]. Never buy those which look as though they have ambitions to become marrows [large summer squash]. Small courgettes [zucchini] will taste infinitely nicer and look far more attractive when served.

**3 tablespoons olive oil**
**1 medium-sized onion, finely chopped**
**1 garlic clove, crushed**
**4 tablespoons dry white wine**
**4 tablespoons water**
**a bouquet garni**
**6 coriander seeds**
**6 black peppercorns**
**1 small lemon**
**salt**
**200-300 g/8-12 oz small courgettes [zucchini]**
**2 tablespoons chopped parsley**

Heat 2 tablespoons of olive oil in a heavy pan or casserole; add the finely chopped onion and the garlic, and sauté until transparent. Add the wine and water, the bouquet garni, coriander seeds, black peppercorns, lemon juice and salt to taste. Bring to the boil and simmer for 5 minutes. Trim the ends of the courgettes [zucchini] and wipe the skins clean with a damp cloth. Do not peel. Quarter them and cut into 5 cm [2 in] segments. Add to the simmering sauce and cook over low heat for 20-25 minutes or until tender but still firm. Transfer the courgettes [zucchini] to a deep serving dish, discard the bouquet garni and pour on the cooking juices. Then allow to cool and chill until ready to serve.

Just before serving, moisten with the remaining olive oil, sprinkle with finely chopped parsley and a little additional lemon juice to taste.

## Chilled seafood appetizer

Try this salad mixed with a French dressing, as in the recipe below, or alternatively coated with a well-flavoured mayonnaise.

**75 g/3 oz/½ cup long grain rice**
**1 L/2 pts/3 pints mussels**
**125 ml/5 fl oz/⅝ cup dry white wine**
**4 tablespoons water**
**1 small onion, finely chopped**
**50 g/2 oz cooked peeled shrimps**
**2 tomatoes, peeled**
**1 tablespoon chopped parsley**
**1 tablespoon grated onion**
**2 tablespoons wine vinegar**
**4-5 tablespoons olive oil**
**salt and freshly ground black pepper.**

Boil the rice in plenty of salted water, until the grains are tender but still firm. Drain thoroughly and set aside to cool. Meanwhile scrub the mussels well, removing the 'beards' and discarding any shells that do not close. Place the mussels in a pan with the wine, water and finely chopped onion. Cover tightly with a lid and cook over high heat, shaking the pan frequently, until the mussels have all opened – about 5-7 minutes.

Remove the mussels from the pan, shaking back any liquid trapped in the shells. Strain the liquid through cheesecloth or a fine sieve lined with kitchen paper. Rinse out the pan and return the liquid to it. Add the shrimps and cook for 10 minutes. Meanwhile remove the mussels from their shells, and discard any which have not opened.

Drain the shrimps and combine with the rice and mussels. Slice the tomatoes and add to the mixture, together with the chopped parsley.

Make a French dressing by combining the grated onion, vinegar and oil with a little salt and pepper. Combine all the ingredients thoroughly together with a fork. Pour over the salad and toss lightly. Chill before serving.

### Avocado and seafood salad

A variety of seafood mixed with avocado makes a wonderfully exotic salad to serve.

**2 anchovy fillets**
**50 g/2 oz cooked, peeled prawns or shrimps**
**2 tablespoons vinaigrette or thick mayonnaise**
**a little grated lemon zest**
**salt**
**freshly ground black pepper**
**1 ripe avocado pear**
**a squeeze of lemon juice**

Remove all the oil from the anchovies by draining them on kitchen paper. Using a pair of scissors, snip the fillets into small pieces. Place them in a mixing bowl.

Add the prawns or shrimps (reserving a few for garnish), mayonnaise or vinaigrette, and lemon zest. Stir to mix and season well. Cut the avocado in half, remove the stone and peel the skin from the flesh. Cut the flesh, sprinkle on the lemon juice then add to the other ingredients in the bowl and mix lightly together.

Transfer the salad to a small serving dish and garnish with a whole prawn or shrimp and a twist of lemon.

### Greek island salad

This Greek salad is traditionally made with Fetta cheese. White Stilton is fairly similar, more widely available and perfectly adequate for this recipe.

**75 g/3 oz Fetta cheese, or white Stilton**
**3 large tomatoes, thinly sliced**
**1 onion, sliced in thin rings**
**6-8 black olives**
**1 medium-sized gherkin, sliced**
**1 teaspoon finely crushed coriander seeds**
**½ teaspoon oregano**
**2 tablespoons olive oil**
**salt**
**freshly ground black pepper**

Cut the cheese into fairly thin strips, about 3.8 cm [1½ in] in length. Place the cheese in a salad bowl, add the tomatoes, olives, and gherkins and mix together. In a small bowl combine the crushed coriander, crushed garlic and oregano with the olive oil, and pour over the salad. Season with salt and freshly ground black pepper and serve with hot fresh bread.

### Salmagundy

Salmagundy is a traditional British salad, popular in the seventeenth and eighteenth centuries, which is built up like a small pyramid, with different, brightly coloured ingredients.

**1 teaspoon vegetable oil**
**½ medium-sized curly endive [chicory], coarse outer leaves removed, washed, shaken dry and shredded**
**450 g/1 lb cooked chicken meat, sliced**

***Below*** *Attractive to look at and delicious to eat, Salmagundy is a traditional British salad. A perfect dish for a party.*

*Above* Bacon slices stuffed with a mixture of mushrooms and onions make a tasty savoury.

**450 g/1 lb lean cooked tongue, sliced**
**6 hard-boiled eggs, separated and finely chopped**
**8 rollmops or pickled herrings, drained**
**2 large tomatoes, quartered**
**1 large lemon, quartered**
**1 large orange, quartered**
**1 small cooked beetroot [beet] finely chopped**
**8 black olives, stoned**
**1 small dill pickle, finely chopped**
**8 tablespoons chopped fresh water-cress**
**200 g/8 oz/1 cup butter, frozen in 1 piece for 'statue' (optional)**

With the oil, lightly grease the outside of a shallow pudding basin or large saucer and place it, inverted, on a large round serving plate.

Sprinkle the endive [chicory] over the saucer. Arrange the chicken slices around the edge of the serving plate and make another slightly smaller circle with the tongue. Make a circle of chopped egg yolks. Arrange the herrings inside the egg yolk circle and place a tomato quarter between each herring. Make a circle with the egg whites and, inside this, arrange the orange and lemon quarters alternately. Sprinkle the beet-root [beet], olives and dill pickle over the basin or saucer. Make a cicle around the outer edge of the plate with the watercress.

Place the plate in the refrigerator and chill for 30 minutes.

Place the butter on a wooden board. Using a small sharp knife, carve the butter into a decorative shape, such as a flower, fruit or bird.

Remove the plate from the refrigerator. Place the butter decoration in the centre of the endive [chicory]. Serve at once.

## Mushroom rolls

Serve the savoury rolls at a buffet party with a fresh watercress salad tossed in French dressing.

20 ROLLS

**125 g/5 oz/$\frac{5}{8}$ cup butter**
**1 medium-sized onion, coarsely chopped**
**200 g/8 oz mushrooms, wiped clean and coarsely chopped**
**$\frac{1}{4}$ teaspoon black pepper**
**1 tablespoon fresh lemon juice**
**50 g/2 oz/1 cup fresh breadcrumbs, soaked in 50 ml/2 fl oz/$\frac{1}{4}$ cup chicken stock**
**1 tablespoon finely chopped fresh parsley**
**20 lean bacon slices, rinds removed**

In a large saucepan, melt 100 g/4 oz /$\frac{1}{2}$ cup of the butter over low heat. When the foam subsides, add the onion and mushrooms. Gently simmer, stirring occasionally, for 5 minutes or until the mushrooms are soft. Remove the pan from the heat.

Preheat the grill [broiler] to high.

Using a slotted spoon, transfer the mushrooms and onion to a large mixing bowl. Add the pepper, lemon juice, breadcrumb mixture and parsley. With a potato masher or fork, mash the ingred-ients together until they form a paste.

Lay the bacon slices out flat. Spread each slice with a little of the paste. Roll up the bacon slices and thread them on to skewers (about four rolls to each skewer). Place the skewers on the grill [broiler], turning them occasionally, cook them for 10 minutes, or until the bacon is crisp.

Serve hot.

In a small saucepan, melt the remaining butter over moderate heat. Remove the pan from the heat and brush the melted butter over the rolls. Place the rolls under the grill [broiler] and grill [broil], turning frequently, for 6 to 8 minutes, or until the bacon is crisp.

Remove the skewers from the grill [broiler] and slide the rolls off the skewers on to a warmed serving dish. Serve at once.

### Sicilian stuffed tomatoes

A tasty dish to serve at a buffet. They may be served either hot or cold.

4 SERVINGS

**8 large firm tomatoes**
**6 tablespoons olive oil**
**2 medium-sized onions, finely chopped**
**1 garlic clove, crushed**
**100 g/4 oz/2 cups fresh breadcrumbs**
**8 anchovy fillets, chopped**
**3 tablespoons black olives, stoned and chopped**
**2 tablespoons chopped fresh parsley**
**2 teaspoons chopped fresh oregano or 1 teaspoon dried oregano**
**3 tablespoons grated Parmesan cheese**
**1 tablespoon butter, cut into 8 pieces**

Preheat the oven to moderate Gas Mark 4, 180°C [350°F].

Place the tomatoes on a board and cut off the tops with a sharp knife. Discard the tops. With a teaspoon, scoop out and discard the seeds, taking care to pierce the skin. Set the tomatoes aside.

In a medium-sized frying pan, heat the oil over moderate heat. When the oil is hot, add the onions and garlic and fry, stirring occasionally, for 5 to 7 minutes or until the onions are soft and translucent but not brown. Remove the pan from the heat and stir in the breadcrumbs, anchovies, olives, parsley and oregano.

Using a teaspoon, fill the tomatoes with the breadcrumb mixture. Place the tomatoes in an ovenproof dish large enough to take them in one layer.

Sprinkle the Parmesan cheese over the stuffed tomatoes and top each one with a piece of butter.

Place the dish in the oven and bake the tomatoes for 20 to 30 minutes or until the tops are lightly browned and the tomatoes are tender but still firm.

Remove the dish from the oven and serve immediately. If you wish to serve the tomatoes cold, allow them to cool in the dish, then chill them in the refrigerator for at least 1 hour before serving.

# STUFFED EGGS

### Portuguese eggs in tomato shells

These are hard-boiled eggs in tomato cases garnished with tomato sauce. It is eaten cold as a first course, or as a party snack.

6 SERVINGS

**6 large firm tomatoes, blanched and peeled**
**1 teaspoon salt**
**½ teaspoon black pepper**
**2 tablespoons olive oil**
**1 small onion, finely chopped**
**2 teaspoons fresh chopped basil or ½ teaspoon dried basil**
**1 tablespoon tomato purée [paste]**
**6 hard-boiled eggs**
**4 tablespoons mayonnaise**
**watercress**

Cut a circle out of the stalk end of each tomato so that there will be an opening big enough to insert an egg. With a teaspoon carefully scoop out the pulp and seeds. Reserve the pulp, seeds and lids. Sprinkle the insides of the scooped-out tomatoes with half the salt and pepper and set aside.

In a small saucepan, heat the oil over moderate heat. When the oil is hot, add the onion and fry, stirring occasionally, for 5 to 7 minutes or until the onion is soft and translucent but not brown. Add the reserved tomato pulp and seeds, the tomato lids, the basil, tomato purée

***Right** Portuguese eggs in tomato shells garnished with watercress make attractive hors d'oeuvres to serve.*

[paste] and the remaining salt and pepper. Reduce the heat to low, cover the pan and simmer for 15 to 20 minutes or until the mixture is thick.

Remove the pan from the heat and set the sauce aside to cool.

Place the tomato shells on a serving dish. Place a hard-boiled egg in each shell. Place the dish in the refrigerator and chill for at least 20 minutes.

When the sauce is cold, stir in the mayonnaise. Transfer the sauce to a small mixing bowl and place it in the refrigerator to chill.

Just before serving, remove the eggs in tomato shells and sauce from the refrigerator. Spoon the sauce over the eggs. Garnish with watercress and serve.

***Above** Tomatoes stuffed with anchovies, herbs and cheese may be served hot or cold as a tempting party dish.*

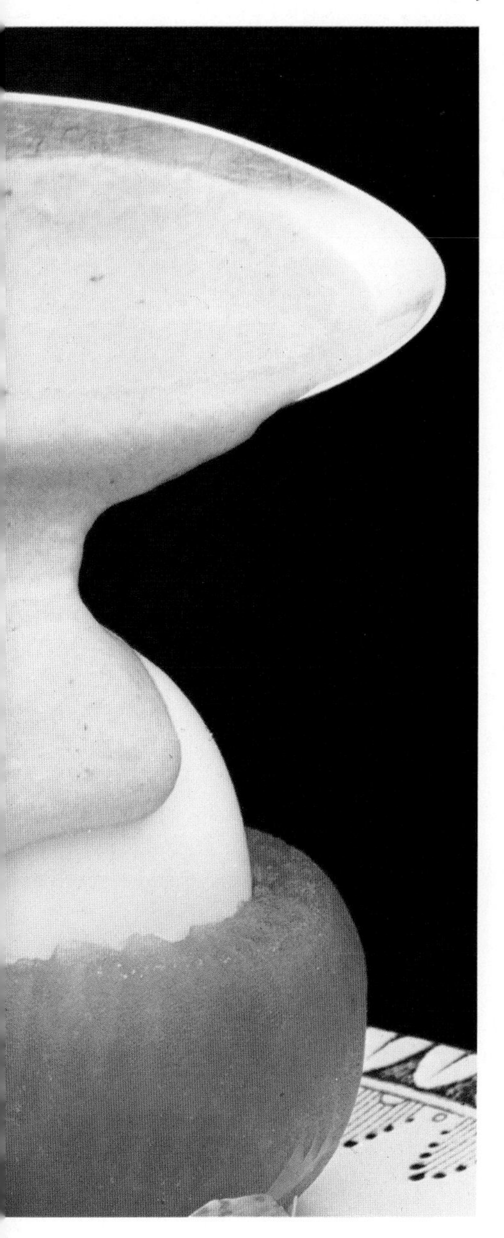

## Eggs stuffed with tuna

Stuffed with a mixture of tuna fish, pickled gherkins and mayonnaise, these eggs make an attractive hors d'oeuvre or part of a cold buffet.

6-12 SERVINGS

**50 g/2 oz/¼ cup butter**
**100 g/4 oz canned tuna fish, drained**
**1 tablespoon lemon juice**
**4 tablespoons mayonnaise**
**¼ teaspoon black pepper**
**½ teaspoon paprika**
**3 small, sweet pickled gherkins, finely chopped**
**12 hard-boiled eggs**
**1 bunch of watercress, washed and shaken dry**

In a medium-sized mixing bowl, mash the butter and tuna fish together with a fork until they are thoroughly combined. Add the lemon juice, mayonnaise, pepper, paprika and gherkins. Combine the ingredients thoroughly and set the bowl aside.

Cut off about 2.5 cm [1 in] of the rounded end of the eggs. Retain these 'lids'. Slice a thin strip from the pointed ends of the eggs so that they will sit flat. Using a teaspoon, carefully remove the egg yolks from the whites, being careful to keep the white intact. Set the whites aside.

Mash the egg yolks into the tuna fish mixture, mixing them in thoroughly. Stuff the egg whites with the tuna and egg yolk mixture. Replace the 'lids' on top of the stuffed eggs.

Arrange the watercress on a large shallow serving dish. Place the eggs, standing upright on the cress. Chill in the refrigerator for 20 minutes before serving.

## Eggs stuffed with ham and herbs

Hard-boiled eggs stuffed with a delicious ham and herb mixture and then fried, eggs stuffed with ham and herbs may be served with a thick tomato and onion sauce.

2 SERVINGS

**4 hard-boiled eggs**

**50 g/2 oz cooked ham finely chopped**
**100 g/4 oz/½ cup butter**
**1 tablespoon chopped chives**
**1 teaspoon dried thyme**
**1 teaspoon Worcestershire sauce**
**2 eggs**
**½ teaspoon salt**
**¼ teaspoon black pepper**
**4 tablespoons dry white breadcrumbs**

Cut the eggs in half, lengthways. Remove the yolks and place them in a medium-sized mixing bowl. Set the white aside. Add the ham, half of the butter, the chives, thyme, Worcestershire sauce, one egg, salt and pepper.

With a wooden spoon, cream the mixture thoroughly until it is smooth.

Spoon the mixture into the egg white halves. Sandwich the halves together to form a whole egg. The halves should not fit tightly together.

In a small bowl, lightly beat the second egg with a fork. Roll the stuffed eggs in the beaten egg and then in the breadcrumbs.

***Below*** *Hard-boiled eggs stuffed with a delicious ham and herb mixture and then fried make a warm, filling dish.*

In a medium-sized frying-pan, melt the remaining butter over moderate heat. Place the stuffed eggs in the pan and fry them for 5 minutes, or until they are golden brown all over.

With a slotted spoon, carefully transfer the stuffed eggs from the pan to a warmed serving dish and serve at once.

## Eggs with tarragon mayonnaise

This is an inexpensive, tasty and attractive dish to serve as part of an hors d'oeuvre or, as a first course for a dinner party.

4 SERVINGS

**2 egg yolks**
**½ teaspoon salt**
**1 teaspoon prepared mustard**
**⅛ teaspoon white pepper**
**200 ml/8 fl oz/1 cup olive oil**
**1 tablespoon tarragon vinegar**
**1 teaspoon chopped fresh tarragon or ¼ teaspoon dried tarragon**
**1 teaspoon chopped fresh chives**
**1½ tablespoons boiling water**
**1 round lettuce outer leaves removed washed and separated into leaves**
**6 hard-boiled eggs, cut in halves, lengthways**
**4 anchovies**
**1 tablespoon chopped parsley**

To make the mayonnaise, place the egg yolks, mustard, salt and pepper in a medium-sized mixing bowl. Using a wire whisk, beat the ingredients until they are thoroughly blended. Add the oil, a few drops at a time, whisking constantly. Do not add the oil too quickly or the mayonnaise will curdle. After the mayonnaise has thickened, the oil may be added more rapidly. Beat in a few drops of vinegar from time to time to prevent the mayonnaise from becoming too thick. When all the oil has been added, stir in the remaining vinegar, tarragon and chives. Add the boiling water and stir to mix. This gives the mayonnaise a better coating consistency. Taste the mayonnaise and add more seasoning and vinegar if necessary.

To serve, place the lettuce leaves on 4 serving plates. Place 3 egg halves, cut side down, arranged like a 3 petalled flower, on the lettuce. Coat the eggs with the mayonnaise. Put one curled anchovy in the centre of each egg 'flower'. Sprinkle the top with the parsley and serve.

Take the pots from the refrigerator. Remove and discard the foil and serve.

### Fish and prawn mousse

This superb mousse is the ideal main dish for a cocktail or buffet party, since it may be prepared well in advance. Alternatively, it may be served as a rich first course.

4-6 SERVINGS

**450 g/1 lb haddock or cod fillets**
**300 g/12 oz prawns or shrimps, shelled**
**1 teaspoon Worcestershire sauce**
**1 teaspoon salt**
**¼ teaspoon white pepper**
**⅛ tablespoon tomato purée [paste]**
**130 ml/5 fl oz/⅝ cup double [heavy] cream, stiffly whipped**
**13 g/ ½ oz gelatine dissolved in 3 tablespoons water**
**1 head lettuce, shredded**

MAYONNAISE

**2 egg yolks, at room temperature**
**½ teaspoon salt**
**¾ teaspoon dry mustard**
**⅛ teaspoon white pepper**

# SEAFOOD

***Above** A perfect dish for a drinks party – potted shrimps or prawns with bread.*

***Below** Crispy fried salmon balls are ideal for a hot buffet dish.*

### Potted shrimps or prawns

A traditional British speciality, potted shrimps are very easy to prepare. White fish is often added to the shrimps or prawns and the mixture may be put into one big dish rather than small individual pots. Serve with thin slices of brown bread and garnish with watercress. Potted shrimps or prawns may be kept for up to a week in the refrigerator.

10 SERVINGS

**125 g/5 oz/⅝ cup butter**
**¼ teaspoon ground mace**
**⅛ teaspoon cayenne pepper**
**½ teaspoon black pepper**
**450 g/1 lb of shrimps or prawns, cooked and shelled**
**75 g/3 oz/⅜ cup clarified butter, melted**

In a large frying pan, melt the butter over moderate heat. When the foam subsides, stir in the mace, cayenne, salt and pepper. Add the shrimps or prawns to the pan and coat them roughly with the seasoned butter. Remove the pan from the heat.

Spoon equal amounts of the mixture into ten small pots, leaving a 6 mm [¼ in] space at the top. Pour 1 tablespoon of the clarified butter into each pot. Cover the pots with aluminium foil and put them in the refrigerator to chill for at least 2 hours.

**250 ml/10 fl oz/1¼ cups olive oil, at room temperature**
**1 tablespoon white wine vinegar or lemon juice**

First prepare the mayonnaise. Place the egg yolks, salt, mustard and pepper in a large mixing bowl. Using a wire whisk, beat the ingredients until they are thoroughly blended. Add the oil, a few drops at a time, whisking constantly. Do not add the oil too quickly or the mayonnaise will curdle. After the mayonnaise has thickened the oil may be added a little more rapidly. Beat in a few drops of lemon juice or vinegar from time to time to prevent the mayonnaise from becoming too thick. When all the oil has been added, stir in the remaining lemon juice or vinegar. Taste for seasoning and add more salt, mustard and vinegar (or lemon juice) if desired. Set the bowl aside.

In a fish steamer, steam fish fillets over moderate heat for 10 to 15 minutes, or until they flake easily when tested with a fork. Allow the fish to cool, then skin the fillets and flake them with a fork. Fold the fish, 200 g/8 oz of the prawns or shrimps, the Worcestershire sauce, salt, pepper, cayenne pepper, tomato purée [paste] and cream into the mayonnaise. Stir the dissolved gelatine into the mayonnaise mixture.

Turn the mixture into a 1 L/40 fl oz/1½ qt mould. Cover the mould and place it in the refrigerator. Leave it for 2 to 3 hours, or until it is set.

To turn the mousse out, quickly dip the mould into hot water. Place a serving dish, inverted, over the mould and reverse the two.

Garnish the mousse with the remaining prawns or shrimps and the lettuce.

## Fish mould

This is a tasty and attractive way of using fish, which makes an attractive centerpiece for a buffet party. The mould is served with a coleslaw dressing and garnished with tomatoes and hard-boiled egg.

2 SERVINGS

**200 g/ 8 oz white fish, cooked, skinned, boned and flaked**

***Below*** *Rich and creamy, fish and prawn mousse makes a lovely centrepiece. Serve garnished with prawns and lettuce.*

**250 ml/10 fl oz/1¼ cups bechamel sauce**
**½ teaspoon salt**
**¼ teaspoon white pepper**
**13 g/½ oz gelatine**
**1 tablespoon double [heavy] cream**
**1 small onion, finely chopped**
**1 tablespoon chopped parsley**
**1 pickled cucumber, finely chopped**
**1 tablespoon chopped pimientoes**
**200 ml/8 fl oz/1 cup coleslaw dressing**
**3 tomatoes, sliced**
**1 hard-boiled egg, sliced**

In a medium-sized mixing bowl, mash the fish and béchamel sauce together with a wooden spoon until the mixture is smooth. Alternatively, the fish and sauce may be puréed in an electric blender. Season with the salt and pepper.

In a cup set in a pan of hot water, dissolve the gelatine in 2 tablespoons of water.

Stir the dissolved gelatine and cream into the fish mixture. Turn the mixture into a 500 ml/20 fl oz/2½ cup mould and place it in the refrigerator. Leave it for 2 to 3 hours, or until it is set.

In a small mixing bowl, combine the onion, parsley, pickled cucumber and pimientoes with the coleslaw dressing.

Run a knife around the edge of the mould and quickly dip it into hot water. Place a large serving dish, inverted, over the mould and reverse the two.

Pour the dressing over the mould and surround it with the tomatoes and the sliced hard-boiled egg.

## Salmon balls

Crunchy salmon balls are just the thing for a hot buffet and, if you wish to make them even more special, serve them with a creamy seafood dip. Instant potato is used here to reduce preparation time and tastes superb.

ABOUT 60 BALLS

**3¾ oz/1¼ cups instant potato**
**300 g/12 oz canned red salmon, drained and finely flaked**
**1 egg, lightly beaten**
**325 g/13 oz/6½ cups fresh breadcrumbs**
**¼ teaspoon cayenne pepper**
**1½ teaspoons salt**
**1 teaspoon black pepper**
**½ teaspoon dried dill**
**1 tablespoon chopped fresh parsley**
**2 eggs, lightly beaten with 4 tablespoons milk**
**sufficient vegetable oil for deep-frying**

Make up the instant potato according to the directions on the packet. Stir in the salmon, egg, 25 g/1 oz/½ cup of the breadcrumbs, the cayenne pepper, salt, black pepper, dill and parsley and beat with a wooden spoon until the ingredients are thoroughly combined.

With generously floured hands, shape heaped teaspoons of the salmon mixture into 2.5 cm [1 in] balls. Reflour your hands after shaping each ball. Set aside.

Place the egg and milk mixture in one dish and the remaining breadcrumbs in another.

Roll the salmon balls first in the egg mixture and then in the breadcrumbs, coating them thoroughly and shaking off any excess. Reshape the salmon balls if necessary. Set aside.

Fill a deep-frying pan one-third full with the oil. Set the pan over moderately high heat and heat the oil until it registers 190°C [375°F] on a deep-fat thermometer or until a small cube of stale bread dropped into the oil turns golden brown in 40 seconds. Reduce the heat to moderate. Carefully lower the salmon balls, about 8 at a time, into the oil and fry them for 2 minutes or until they are crisp and golden brown. Remove the salmon balls from the oil and drain them on kitchen paper towels. Keep them warm while you fry and drain the remaining salmon balls in the same way.

## Smoked trout pâté

Simple and easy to make, smoked trout pâté makes the perfect hors d'oeuvre, served with hot toast and butter. Alternatively, serve it as part of a cold buffet.

6 SERVINGS

**1 kg/2 lb smoked trout, skinned, boned and flaked**
**100 ml/4 fl oz/½ cup single [light] cream**
**100 g/4 oz cream cheese**
**2 tablespoons prepared horseradish sauce**
**2 tablespoons lemon juice**
**1 teaspoon black pepper**
**1 tablespoon chopped fresh parsley**
**3 thin lemon slices, halved**

Place the fish and cream in the jar of an electric blender at high speed until the mixture forms a purée. Alternatively pound the fish with the cream, a little at a time, in a mortar with a pestle until the mixture forms a smooth paste.

Spoon the purée into a medium-sized mixing bowl. With a wooden spoon, beat in the cream cheese, horseradish sauce, lemon juice, pepper and parsley. Continue beating the mixture until it is smooth and creamy. Spoon the pâté into individual ramekin dishes. Smooth the top down with the back of a spoon and garnish with the lemon half slices.

Place the dishes in the refrigerator to chill for 1 hour before serving.

## Bacon and liver rolls

These tasty and inexpensive appetizers or hors d'oeuvres will brighten any buffet.

20 ROLLS

**250 ml/10 fl oz/1¼ cups water**
**½ teaspoon salt**
**200 g/8 oz chicken livers**
**2 hard-boiled eggs**
**2 tablespoons finely chopped onion**
**2 teaspoons chopped parsley**

¼ teaspoon salt
freshly ground black pepper
2 tablespoons butter, softened
½ teaspoon lemon juice
1 teaspoon brandy
10 bacon slices, cut in halves

In a medium-sized saucepan, bring the water to boil. Add the salt and the chicken livers. Boil them for 7 minutes or until they are just cooked. Drain the livers.

Using the back of a spoon, rub the hard-boiled eggs and the chicken livers through a fine sieve into a bowl. Add the onions, parsley, salt, 4 grindings of pepper, butter, lemon juice and brandy. Stir the mixture well and chill it in the refrigerator for 30 minutes.

Spread the chicken liver mixture on the strips of bacon. Roll up the bacon strips and put a wooden cocktail stick through the centre of each one. Place the rolls under a fairly hot grill [broiler] and, turning them occasionally, cook them for 10 minutes, or until the bacon is crisp. Serve hot.

*Below Rolls of bacon filled with a rich liver mixture makes a tasty snack for a buffet party.*

## Avocado with jellied consommé

An unusual dish for a buffet, jellied tomato consommé piled into avocado halves and garnished with watercress is elegant but inexpensive.

6 SERVINGS

**350 g/14 oz canned peeled tomatoes**
**1 onion, sliced**
**½ teaspoon dried basil**
**4 allspice berries**
**1 bay leaf**
**½ oz gelatine**
**300 ml/12 fl oz/1½ cups condensed consommé**
**½ teaspoon salt**
**½ teaspoon black pepper**
**3 avocados**
**juice of ½ lemon**

Put the tomatoes, onion, basil, allspice and bay leaf in a medium-sized pan and bring to the boil. Lower the heat and simmer uncovered for 40 minutes. Strain through a sieve into a bowl.

In a cup, mix the gelatine with 4 tablespoons of the hot tomato liquid. When it has dissolved add it to the bowl.

Warm the consommé and add it with the salt and pepper to the tomato liquid. Mix well and pour the mixture into a shallow dish. Chill in the refrigerator until it sets.

Cut the avocados in half lengthways and remove the stones. Sprinkle the cut surfaces with the lemon juice.

# QUICHES

## Asparagus quiche

A delicately flavoured and coloured dish, asparagus quiche may be served hot or cold, with a lettuce salad.

4-6 SERVINGS

**22.5 cm [9 in] flan case [pie crust] made with shortcrust pastry**
FILLING
**150 g/6 oz cooked ham, chopped**

**100 ml/4 fl oz/$\frac{1}{2}$ cup single [light] cream**
**75 ml/3 fl oz/$\frac{3}{8}$ cup milk**
**3 eggs**
**25 g/1 oz/$\frac{1}{4}$ cup Cheddar cheese, grated**
**$\frac{1}{4}$ teaspoon salt**
**$\frac{1}{2}$ teaspoon white pepper**
**12 asparagus tips, cooked and drained**

Preheat the oven to Gas Mark 6, 200°C [400°F]. Place the case on a baking sheet.

Cover the base of the flan case [pie crust] with the chopped ham and set aside.

In a medium-sized mixing bowl, combine the cream, milk, eggs, grated cheese, salt and pepper and beat well to blend.

Pour the mixture over the ham. Arrange the asparagus tips, pointed ends toward the centre, around the edge of the filling.

Place the baking sheet in the centre of the oven. Bake the quiche for 35 to 40 minutes or until the filling is set and firm and golden brown on top.

Remove the baking sheet from the

***Above*** *Avocado halves filled with a jellied tomato consommé is an elegant dish.*

***Below*** *Asparagus quiche really tastes marvellous for a different party dish.*

oven and serve the quiche at once, if you are serving it hot. Otherwise, allow it to cool.

## Mushroom quiche

A marvellously tasty dish, mushroom quiche may be served either hot or cold.

4-6 SERVINGS

**22.9 cm [9 in] flan case [pie crust] made with shortcrust pastry**

***Below*** *A simple but appetizing mixture of tomatoes and courgettes [zucchini], this flan is delicious served with a green salad.*

FILLING

**50 g/2 oz/¼ cup butter**
**2 shallots, finely chopped**
**450 g/1 lb button mushrooms, wiped clean and thinly sliced**
**¼ teaspoon salt**
**¼ teaspoon white pepper**
**¼ teaspoon grated nutmeg**
**100 ml/4 fl oz/½ cup single [light] cream**
**3 eggs**
**50 g/2 oz/½ cup Cheddar cheese, grated**

Preheat the oven to Gas Mark 6, 200°C [400°F]. Place the flan case [pie crust] on a baking sheet and set aside.

In a large frying pan, melt the butter over moderate heat. When the foam subsides, add the shallots and cook, stirring occasionally, for 3 to 4 minutes or until they are soft and translucent but not brown. Add the mushrooms to the pan and cook, stirring occasionally, for 3 minutes. Remove the pan from the heat and stir in the salt, pepper and nutmeg. Set aside.

In a medium-sized mixing bowl, combine the cream, eggs and grated cheese and beat well to blend.

*Left A mouthwatering dessert made with a fabulous selection of exotic fruits, tropical fruit salad is superb.*

Add the cream mixture to the mushrooms, stirring constantly until they are well blended.

Pour the mixture into the flan case [pie crust] and place the baking sheet in the centre of the oven. Bake the quiche for 25 to 30 minutes or until the filling is set and firm and golden brown on top.

Remove the baking sheet from the oven and serve the quiche at once, if you are serving it hot.

## Courgette [zucchini] and tomato quiche

A delightful combination of courgettes [zucchini] and tomatoes makes this quiche an extra special dish. Serve hot or cold, either as a first course or, with garlic bread and a mixed green salad, as a delicious lunch or light supper.

4-6 SERVINGS

**22.5 cm [9 in] flan case [pie crust] made with shortcrust pastry**
FILLING
**50 g/2 oz/¼ cup butter**
**2 garlic cloves, crushed**
**4 courgettes [zucchini], trimmed and sliced**
**1 teaspoon salt**
**1 teaspoon black pepper**
**½ teaspoon dried oregano**
**100 ml/4 fl oz/½ cup single [light] cream**
**3 eggs**
**50 g/2 oz/½ cup Cheddar cheese, grated**
**5 small tomatoes, blanched, peeled and thinly sliced**

Preheat the oven to Gas Mark 6, 200°C [400°F]. Place the flan case [pie crust] on a baking sheet and set aside.

In a large frying pan, melt the butter over moderate heat. When the foam subsides, add the garlic and cook, stirring frequently, for 1 minute. Add the courgettes [zucchini] and half of the salt and pepper. Cook, stirring and turning occasionally, for 8 to 10 minutes or until the courgettes [zucchini] are lightly browned. Remove the pan from the heat and stir in the remaining salt and pepper and the oregano, mixing well to blend.

In a medium-sized mixing bowl, combine the cream, eggs and grated cheese and beat well to blend.

Arrange the courgettes [zucchini] and tomato slices in concentric circles in the flan case [pie crust].

Pour the cream mixture over the courgettes [zucchini] and tomatoes.

Place the baking sheet in the centre of the oven and bake the quiche for 35 to 40 minutes or until golden brown on top.

Remove the baking sheet from the oven and serve the quiche at once, if you are serving it hot.

# DESSERTS

## Tropical fruit salad

Tropical fruit salad is an exotic, colourful and fragrant dessert. It is quick to prepare and delightful to serve at a buffet party. Serve it either on its own or with fresh cream or ice-cream.

8 SERVINGS

**1 large pineapple**
**1 large orange, peeled, pith removed and cut into segments**
**2 bananas, peeled and sliced**
**100 g/ 4 oz black grapes, halved and seeded**
**6 fresh passion fruit, tops removed and the pulp squeezed out**
**1 melon, peeled, seeded and chopped**
**400 g/16 oz canned pawpaw**
**400 g/16 oz canned guavas**
**juice of 1 orange**
**juice of 1 lemon**
**100 ml/4 fl oz/½ cup orange-flavoured liqueur**

With a sharp knife, carefully cut off the top and a thin slice of the bottom of the pineapple. Discard the base of the pineapple but retain the top. Remove the flesh from the peel, leaving a 1.3 cm

[$\frac{1}{2}$ in] thick shell. Set the pineapple shell aside.

Remove and discard the core from the pineapple flesh. Cut the flesh into small pieces and place them in a large mixing bowl.

Add the orange, bananas, grapes, passion fruit, melon and pawpaw to the bowl. Strain the guavas through a wire strainer placed over a small mixing bowl and reserve the can juice. Add the guavas to the other fruits and set aside.

Add the orange and lemon juice and orange-flavoured liqueur to the can juice and stir well. Set aside.

Place the reserved pineapple shell, upright, in the centre of a large serving dish. Spoon two-thirds of the fruit mixture around the base of the pineapple. Pour the orange-flavoured liqueur mixture into the pineapple shell. Replace the reserved pineapple top and chill the dish in the refrigerator for 30 minutes or until required.

## White grape and ginger syllabub

An unusual and refreshing dessert, white grape and ginger syllabub is the perfect dish to serve at a drinks or buffet party.

6 SERVINGS

**1 kg/2 lb seedless white grapes, with 6 grapes reserved, halved**
**200 g/8 oz/2 cups crushed ginger biscuits [cookies]**
**4 egg whites, stiffly beaten**
**200 g/8 oz/1 cup castor [fine] sugar**
**250 ml/10 fl oz/1$\frac{1}{4}$ cups white wine**
**juice of $\frac{1}{2}$ lemon**
**375 ml/15 fl oz/1$\frac{7}{8}$ cups double [heavy] cream**
**100 g/4 oz/1 cup slivered almonds, toasted**

Arrange one-quarter of the grapes on the bottom of a medium-sized serving bowl. Cover with one-quarter of the ginger biscuit [cookie] crumbs. Continue making layers in this way until the grapes and the ginger crumbs are used up. Set aside.

Place the beaten egg whites in a medium-sized mixing bowl. Beat in one-quarter of the sugar. Using a metal spoon, fold in the remaining sugar. Pour over the wine and lemon juice and stir the ingredients carefully until they are thoroughly combined. Set aside.

Pour the cream into a large mixing bowl and, using wire whisk or rotary beater, beat the cream until it is thick but not stiff. Using a metal spoon, fold the egg white mixture into the cream. Pour the cream over the fruit and biscuit [cookie] mixture and place in the refrigerator to chill for 2 hours.

Arrange the reserved grapes on top and sprinkle over the almonds. Serve immediately.

***Above** Cool and refreshing, syllabub is a perfect dessert for a party.*

## Trebujena grapefruit cocktail

A refreshing first course from Spain, Trebujena grapefruit cocktail.

6 SERVINGS

**6 small grapefruit**
**250 g/10 oz shelled frozen shrimps, thawed**
**200 g/8 oz frozen crabmeat, thawed and cartilage removed**
**150 g/6 oz smoked salmon, cut into thin strips**
**2 medium-sized tomatoes, finely chopped**
**2 garlic cloves, crushed**
**1 large green pepper, white pith removed, seeded and finely chopped**
**6 small flat lettuce leaves, washed and shaken dry**
**1 teaspoon paprika**

DRESSING

**150 ml/6 fl oz/$\frac{3}{4}$ cup mayonnaise**
**2 tablespoons double [heavy] cream**
**1 tablespoon fresh lemon juice**
**1 teaspoon salt**
**$\frac{1}{2}$ teaspoon black pepper**
**$\frac{1}{8}$ teaspoon cayenne pepper**

Using a sharp knife, cut the tops off the grapefruits and discard. With a sharp-edged teaspoon, scoop out the flesh, seeds and most of the white pith. Be careful not to break the grapefruit shells. Set the shells aside.

Place 4 tablespoons of the grapefruit flesh, finely chopped, in a medium-sized mixing bowl. Reserve the remainder for future use. Add the dressing ingredients and beat well with a wooden spoon until they are thoroughly combined. Add the shrimps, crabmeat, salmon, tomatoes, garlic and green pepper. Stir the mixture well to coat thoroughly the salad ingredients with the dressing.

Place the lettuce leaves on six individual serving plates. Place a grapefruit shell on each lettuce leaf. Divide the fish mixture equally among the grapefruit shells and sprinkle over the paprika.

Chill for 30 minutes before serving.

# BASIC RECIPES

## Mayonnaise

MAKES 250 ML/10 FL OZ/1¼ CUPS

**2 egg yolks**
**1 teaspoon salt**
**½ teaspoon sugar**
**1 teaspoon English mustard**
**freshly ground white pepper**
**250 ml/10 fl oz/1¼ cups olive oil**
**3 tablespoons lemon juice**

Make sure all the ingredients are at room temperature.

Put the two egg yolks into a bowl and mix them thoroughly with the salt, sugar, English mustard and plenty of the freshly ground white pepper.

Add the olive oil drop by drop, letting it run down the sides of the bowl and beating well all the time until the mixture begins to thicken. Then add the oil a little faster, but be careful not to curdle the mayonnaise.

When half the oil is used up add the 1 tablespoon of lemon juice. Add the rest when all the oil has been used up and the mayonnaise is really thick. Taste and adjust the seasoning if necessary.

## Aioli

**2 egg yolks**
**½ teaspoon salt**
**½ teaspoon sugar**
**½ teaspoon dry mustard**
**1½ tablespoons vinegar**
**200 ml/8 fl oz/1 cup olive oil**
**2 cloves of garlic, crushed**

Proceed to make the aioli as the mayonnaise. Mix the egg yolks with the salt, sugar, mustard, 1 tablespoon of vinegar and the crushed garlic. Beat well and add the olive oil a little at a time, making sure it has been absorbed before adding more. When all the oil has been used up add the rest of the vinegar.

## Béchamel sauce

MAKES 250ML/10 FL OZ/1¼ CUPS

**1 small onion, peeled**
**1 small carrot, peeled**
**250 ml/10 fl oz/1¼ cups milk**
**¼ teaspoon ground mace**
**1 small bay leaf**
**4 peppercorns**
**2 cloves**
**25 g/1 oz/2 tablespoons butter**
**3 tablespoons flour**

Place the onion and carrot in a saucepan with the milk, mace, bay leaf, peppercorns and cloves. Bring to the boil then remove from the heat, cover and set aside to infuse for about 15 minutes. Strain.

Melt the butter in a saucepan. Stir in the flour and cook gently for 30 seconds. Remove from the heat and add the infused milk a little at a time, mixing well between each addition. Bring to the boil, stirring continuously until the mixture thickens. Use as required.

## Beurre manié

Beurre manié refers to a paste mixture of equal parts of flour and butter used as a thickening agent.

To make beurre manié, in a saucer blend 2 tablespoons of butter with 4 of flour together with a wooden spoon. With your fingertips, form them into small balls and one by one, whisk them into the hot liquid to be thickened with a wire whisk. Bring the mixture to the simmering point, still stirring, and simmer for 1 to 2 minutes to completely absorb the butter. If the liquid needs additional thickening, add more beurre manié.

# INDEX